Making Your Own

GREETING CARDS
& GIFT WRAP

Making Your Own

GREETING CARDS & GIFT WRAP

More Than 50 Step-by-Step PAPERCRAFTING PROJECTS for Every Occasion

Vivienne Bolton

COMPANIONHOUSE
BOOKS

Dedication

For Michael, Zolii, Bianca, Sophie, Chloe, Ben and Joshua.

Acknowledgments

Special thanks to the editor of the first edition of this book, Clare Hubbard, who is always calm, supportive, and organized. Thanks also to Shona Wood, whose photography complements my work so well, Rosemary Wilkinson, and Corin and Chloe for dreaming up names for the cards. Thanks also to Fiskars UK Ltd (Newlands Avenue, Bridgend CF31 2XA) for supplying equipment for use in this book.

Making Your Own Greeting Cards & Gift Wrap

CompanionHouse Books™ is an imprint of Fox Chapel Publishers International Ltd.

Project Team
Vice President—Content: Christopher Reggio
Editor: Colleen Dorsey
Copy Editor: Anthony Regolino
Design: Llara Pazdan
Index: Elizabeth Walker

All text and card designs: Vivienne Bolton
Photographer: Shona Wood
Template illustrations: Stephen Dew

ISBN 978-1-62008-346-8

Library of Congress Cataloging-in-Publication Data

Names: Bolton, Vivienne, author.
Title: Making your own greeting cards & gift wrap / Vivienne Bolton.
Description: Mount Joy [Pennsylvania] : CompanionHouse Books, [2019] |
  Includes index.
Identifiers: LCCN 2018039282 (print) | LCCN 2018039657 (ebook) | ISBN
  9781620083475 (e-book) | ISBN 9781620083468 (pbk.)
Subjects: LCSH: Greeting cards. | Gift wraps.
Classification: LCC TT872 (ebook) | LCC TT872 .B65 2019 (print) | DDC
  745.594/1--dc23
LC record available at https://lccn.loc.gov/2018039282

This book has been published with the intent to provide accurate and authoritative information in regard to the subject matter within. While every precaution has been taken in the preparation of this book, the author and publisher expressly disclaim any responsibility for any errors, omissions, or adverse effects arising from the use or application of the information contained herein.

Fox Chapel Publishing
903 Square Street
Mount Joy, PA 17552

Fox Chapel Publishers International Ltd.
7 Danefield Road, Selsey (Chichester)
West Sussex PO20 9DA, U.K.

www.facebook.com/companionhousebooks

We are always looking for talented authors. To submit an idea, please send a brief inquiry to acquisitions@foxchapelpublishing.com.

Printed and bound in Singapore
22 21 20 19   2 4 6 8 10 9 7 5 3 1

INTRODUCTION

I have a clear memory of sitting at a newspaper-covered table in my grandmother's sewing room surrounded by scissors, tape, shiny candy wrappers, and a pad of deckle-edged writing paper. I was squeezing runny, brown glue through an orange rubber lid with a slit in it onto a silver doily. I couldn't have been more than six or seven years old when I proudly presented that birthday card to my grandfather.

I haven't changed much since. I still love paper—be it gift wrap, brightly decorated foil candy wrappers, handmade paper, or a child's rainbow-colored writing pad. My range of adhesives has certainly improved. I am now the proud owner of a wide variety of tools and craft materials and I've tried just about every craft there is, but inside I am still that little girl getting a thrill from creativity.

I have thoroughly enjoyed designing the cards and gift wrap for this book. So many different things—colors, textures, materials, and memories of places, friends, and family—have inspired the designs. Some of the cards were originally made with specific friends or family members in mind: for example, Memories (see page 74) was made as a Mother's Day card for my mother, and Magic Number (see page 160) was inspired by the theme we thought up for my youngest grandson's birthday party.

I have particularly enjoyed coordinating gift wrap and greeting cards. It has given me the opportunity to make good use of stamps and stencils. There's something extremely satisfying about a group of cards, tags, bags, pouches, and boxes that all match. It's also an interesting way of developing your design skills.

I am fortunate to have an amazingly well-stocked craft shop just a short drive from my home, along with a variety of art material shops, department stores, and cake-decorating shops (yes, you read that correctly; they are a great source of material for the card maker) in my local town. Experience has taught me to always keep my eyes open when searching for inspiration, new materials, and information.

I store anything that I think might be useful one day, and with card making as a hobby, I have the perfect excuse to save almost everything. In fact, my stock of craft materials is only limited by my available storage space. Get into the habit of looking at everything as a potential material for use on a card; you'll surprise yourself with the ideas that come to you.

Be inspired by the designs in this book, and use them as a springboard from which to create your own designs. I hope you get as much pleasure from using this book as I had from designing and making the projects.

Best wishes,

Vivienne Bolton

Contents

Special Occasions

Time to Celebrate

Galleries

Templates

Index

hen starting any new hobby, equipping yourself with the basic tools and materials is part of the fun. This is particularly the case with card making, as there are so many wonderful things now available for the card maker to buy. Start small with good-quality cutting equipment, a selection of paper and cardstock (card), and adhesive tape and glue. As you work your way through the projects in this book, you will find that your collection of tools and materials will grow and that your scrap box of bits and pieces will begin to burst with all of the interesting things that you've found.

Search out good suppliers, both local stores and mail-order companies (a reliable mail-order supplier is invaluable). As well as checking out craft suppliers, look in cake decorating shops and art material outlets. Small stores are often better, as they have time for customers and often specialize in certain areas.

If you are fortunate enough to have the space, create a permanent work surface for yourself and devote a cabinet or shelf to the storage of your materials. If space is an issue in your house, make yourself a portable "craft workshop"—a couple of boxes to hold materials and equipment, along with a protective surface cover and a large cutting mat. Decorate and label your storage boxes, and keep things filed for easy access. I can't emphasize enough how important it is to keep your tools and materials in good order and condition. No matter how much time you spend making a card, it won't look good if the paper is creased or marked or your craft knife is blunt.

This section of the book examines all of the materials and equipment that you will need to complete the projects in this book. Also demonstrated here are the basic techniques of scoring, template tracing, and folding. There are sections on card design, decorating envelopes, and making gift wrap. By the time you finish reviewing these pages, you will be totally prepared to tackle any project in this book.

GETTING STARTED

"Cardstock" is the US term and "card" is the UK term for thicker crafting paper. The term "cardstock" is used throughout this book.

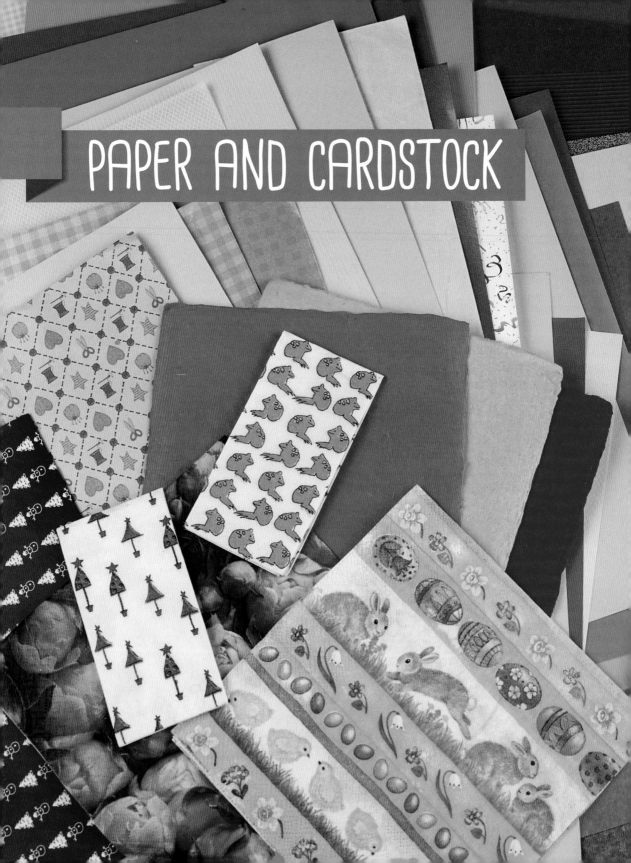

PAPER AND CARDSTOCK

A wide range of paper and cardstock is available in good stationery and craft stores, as well as through mail-order suppliers. Paper and cardstock comes in standard sizes. In the United States, common sizes include letter (8½" x 11" / 216 x 279mm) and half letter (5½" x 8½" / 140 x 216mm), which is half the height of letter (easy to cut yourself by cutting a piece of letter paper in half); many square sizes are also common. In Europe, paper is sized in the A series, with A4 (8¼" x 11 ¹¹⁄₁₆" / 210 x 297mm) being the standard size for most letterhead and copy/printer paper, the equivalent to US letter paper. A5 (5 ¹³⁄₁₆" x 8¼" / 148 x 210mm), the equivalent to US half letter, is also common. Although I occasionally purchase paper in larger sheets, I find that letterhead and smaller sheets are easiest to handle and are less likely to be damaged in transit or storage. Most of the projects in this book start out with letter/A4 or half letter/A5 papers. It doesn't matter which one you use; just be consistent and **don't mix US system paper sizes with European system paper sizes,** as they are very close in size but not identical.

An Important Note to US Readers

All the cards in this book were originally made with European paper sizes. As A4 paper and A5 paper are slightly longer than US letter and half letter paper, a difference could be visible in the final product if half letter paper is used instead of A5 paper whenever A5 paper is called for as a card base. *For this reason, in many projects in this book, US readers are instructed to cut letter size paper close to the UK A5 size when creating the card base.* Alternatively, US readers can use half letter paper and adjust the size of the decorative elements to suit the slightly smaller size of a card made with the US paper size—but this will usually take longer and result in a squarer card. Also, any time half letter/A5 paper is called for in a materials list, any reader can simply cut from a larger letter/A4 paper, especially if you already have a stash of paper to choose from.

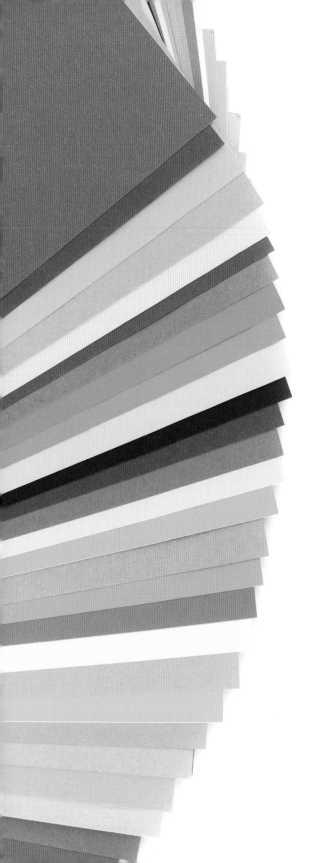

From the finest tissue to the thickest cardstock, paper and cardstock are available in almost any shade, weight, quality, or texture. I always have a selection of textured and plain white and cream cardstock on hand, as many designs seem to begin best with a white or cream card base. I also often prepare colored card bases and store them in a special basket filed by color.

Consider the texture and thickness of cardstock when choosing sheets for particular projects. While you will need good-quality cardstock for a card base, paper or thin cardstock is suitable for framing a central feature or for creating layers. I purchase sheets of gift wrap whenever I see something that inspires me, and I save used Christmas and birthday wrapping paper—you never know when something will be useful. Gift wrap can be used as a card base, but you will need to back it first to give it some stability.

Paper and cardstock are the key raw materials of card making, so you will need a good storage system. Store paper flat and divide it by size, color, and quality so that it is easy to find when you're working. If paper becomes creased, you can try smoothing it with a warm iron to restore it to near-perfect condition. Never throw scraps of paper and cardstock away— keep a small box of scraps, as they will be useful later for small projects, collages, and layering.

Construction (sugar) paper

This thick, slightly textured paper comes in muted shades and is one of the cheapest papers available. Construction (sugar) paper is best used as a feature rather than a card base.

Corrugated cardstock and paper

This comes in a variety of corrugation patterns and colors. Use it as a card base or in layering. It is also great for making your own cutouts and motifs, and is effective wrapping for cylindrical-shaped objects.

Handmade paper

Handmade paper is available in everything from soft pastel colors to rich, jewel-like shades. The prettiest papers often have flower petals and leaves embedded in them, giving the papers a wonderful texture. Handmade paper comes in a variety of weights, the thicker of which can be used as card bases. Used in layering or to create backgrounds, handmade paper always creates an interesting feature.

Mulberry paper

This is a light, opaque paper that is handmade from mulberry leaves and contains strands of silk. It is available in many colors, is lightweight, and has a slight textured pattern that can be very impactful when used creatively. Mulberry paper can be attached with spray adhesive.

Corrugated cardstock and patterned paper

Metallic paper

These papers are good highlighters and are effective when used to create borders, frames, and cutouts. They come in a variety of finishes—some muted, others glossy. Metallic paper is easily damaged, so it should be stored properly. It is advisable to put layers of tissue paper between each sheet.

Translucent paper

I love the softness and depth you can create with these papers. When layered on other colors or white, they bring a special quality to cards. Translucent paper can be used as a card base, but it should be backed with cardstock to give it some substance.

Vellum

This is a semi-opaque paper, available plain or patterned. It is very useful for layering.

Plastic sheeting

Plastic sheeting (or acetate sheeting) is a versatile, heavyweight translucent plastic. It is very flexible, so it is useful for pop-ups. Attach with double-sided tape or glue dots. If you can't find acetate sheeting, substitute with a suitable weight of vellum.

Patterned paper

Commercially available patterned paper and gift wrap can be the basis of wonderful cards. You can use them for backgrounds or cut motifs from them. Make bags and cover gift boxes with gift wrap to create coordinated gift sets. Store gift wrap rolled or flat.

Table napkins and paper tissues

These are a delightful decorative material source. I have found paper tissues printed with frogs, umbrellas, and roses, and table napkins are available in a wide variety of designs. Use spray adhesive to attach these materials to cards, and don't forget to separate the patterned layer out first.

Angel hair paper

This is a stiff, gauzy paper/fabric that is useful for layers. It looks a bit like individual fibers or cotton candy pressed into a sheet. It's a specialty product that you may have to hunt for. If you can't find it, you can try making your own by ironing hot fix fibers (sometimes called Angelina or fantasy fibers), used in sewing/quilting, into a sheet. Follow the manufacturer's instructions.

The notes on pages 10–27 are general information on the variety of products and materials that are available to the card maker. You should always follow the manufacturer's instructions for the specific products that you buy.

Angel hair paper

Pens, Pencils, and Paints

Pens

I always have a good handwriting pen and a black or blue fine-tip pen on hand. Fine-tip pens are very useful and come in a wide range of colors.

Pencils

Pencils are graded by the hardness of the lead. HB is the all-purpose pencil—the lead is neither especially hard nor soft. If you want a fine line, choose an H or HH pencil; if you need a soft, dark line, then go for a 3B or 4B pencil. I always keep a selection of pencils. My favorite pencil is a mechanical one that contains a soft lead. It is easy to erase and is lovely to write with and to draw out rough designs.

Markers

These are useful for creating designs on plastic sheeting or vellum. A double-ended fine-/broad-point marker in black is my favorite. I use a marker when transferring patterns, as the marks are clear, clean, and easy to see.

Pencil

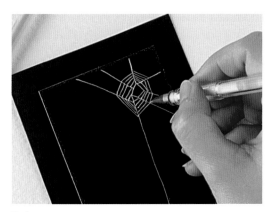
Gel pen

3D paint

Silver and gold pens

I find fine-nib silver and gold pens very useful when writing on cards, particularly on black paper or cardstock. Liquid silver and gold pens are also useful, but test them out on your paper first, as the ink sometimes bleeds. It is important to replace the lid immediately after use.

Gel pens

These highly versatile pens are lovely to decorate cards with. The quality of the ink is very good and the colors are amazing. You can write with one gel pen over another, and they are effective on light and dark papers.

Felt-tip pens

Felt-tip pens are always useful because they come in such a variety of thicknesses and colors—and are an economical option. They are good for marking up edgings; also try creating rainbow borders with different shades. Use them for highlighting, writing messages inside cards, and to ink up intricate rubber stamp designs in place of an inkpad.

3D paint

3D paint can be used as a paint or a glue. Use it to decorate, embellish, or attach. It is great for highlighting, patterns, and corner features. It comes in a rainbow of colors. You can even create a gem effect using colored, translucent 3D paints.

Add dimension and bling at the same time by using metallic 3D paint to embellish.

Cutting and Scoring Equipment

Scissors

Make sure you have small and large paper scissors, fine-tipped scissors for cutouts and other intricate work, and scissors with a patterned edge. Reserve a pair of scissors specifically for cutting fabric. My Fiskars non-stick scissors are one of my most useful tools. I use them for cutting glued surfaces and sticky tape.

Craft knife

A sharp craft knife is essential for cutting neat edges. Great care should be taken when using a craft knife—always use a metal ruler, work on a cutting mat, and don't cut toward your body. Replace the safety lid after use and keep the knife in a safe place, well out of the reach of children.

Cutting mat

Invest in a cutting mat marked with clear measure lines.

Stylus

Use a stylus to ensure that a neat fold line is scored on paper and cardstock.

Rulers and measuring

Buy a metal ruler for cutting against and a clear plastic ruler for taking measurements. A triangle/set square is essential for drawing accurate right angles.

Shape cutters and templates

I find shape-cutting tools and templates extremely useful and often wonder how I managed without them. They make cutting out shaped windows and frames so much easier. Once you have mastered the technique of using the tools, cutting squares, circles, ovals, and rectangles becomes quick and easy. Always cut on a board or a mat. Practice on scrap paper and cardstock in order to produce good finished pieces. I have used these tools throughout the book, but don't worry if you don't have them; you can just cut the shapes using scissors or a craft knife. I have included templates where appropriate.

ADHESIVES

Keep a selection of different adhesives at hand. Always replace lids and store them correctly.

White glue (PVA glue)

This glue becomes transparent when dry and is useful for attaching paper to cardstock or cardstock to cardstock. I transfer a quantity of white glue to a small squeeze applicator for ease of use. I find this incredibly useful when small quantities of glue are necessary; the narrow applicator tube is easy to keep clear and covered.

Glue stick

A glue stick is a useful alternative to white glue or adhesive tape. Keep the glue stick clean and always replace the lid to prevent the glue from drying out.

Spray adhesive (aerosol glue)

This kind of adhesive is useful when gluing tissue paper, mulberry paper, fabric, or opaque paper. When using spray adhesive, I always use what I call a "glue box." This is a cardboard carton approximately 16" (40cm) square. Place the item to be sprayed in the base of the box. Spray it with adhesive, then close the lid of the box to minimize the inhalation of fumes and glue particles. Remove the sprayed item after a few minutes. Always follow the manufacturer's instructions for the specific type of glue that you buy.

Glue pen

This is perfect for attaching decorative motifs and other small items. When a little sparkle is required, draw lines or patterns or write text with the glue pen and then sprinkle glitter over the glue. For a raised finish, sprinkle with embossing powder and fix with a precision heat tool (see page 25).

Glitter glue

Useful as an embellishment, glitter glue can also be used to attach acetate decoratively.

Adhesive tape

Often simply called tape, this comes in a selection of widths. A good, clear, low-tack tape is very useful.

Double-sided tape

Double-sided tape is wonderful. I love it. You will see how much I love it by how many times I've used it in the projects in this book! Quick and easy to use, double-sided tape comes in a variety of widths and is also available in dispensers that save you the time of cutting little pieces. Use double-sided tape instead of glue for a clean finish.

3D tape

This is a double-sided tape with an added spongy layer, enabling you to create raised pictures or embellishments.

Glue dots

These are excellent when a 3D effect is required. They are also good for attaching buttons and other oddball items. Be careful, as they are very sticky!

STAMPS AND PUNCHES

Stamps

Stamps are available in a huge variety of styles and designs; some even have messages on them. Some are extremely versatile, others you may use only once. Use stamps to create your own motifs and borders. Keep your stamps clean; wash them in warm, soapy water or use stamp cleaner.

Colored inkpads

Use colored inkpads or felt-tip pens to color rubber stamps.

Embossing pads

These can be clear or colored. You simply stamp your design onto the card and sprinkle it with embossing powder.

Embossing pen

Use an embossing pen along with embossing powder for freehand embossing. Do not use regular felt-tip pens, as their ink dries too quickly.

Embossing powders

Embossing powders used with stamps are such fun. Always sprinkle embossing powder over a sheet of scrap paper, shake the project to remove any excess powder, and return any excess powder to the container for reuse.

Precision heat tool

A heat tool is necessary to set embossing powder. These tools get extremely hot, so do take care. Keep your hands and the paper or cardstock that is being heated a safe distance from the heat source (try holding the paper with tweezers or tongs). Take care not to singe the paper. Always follow the manufacturer's instructions.

Homemade stamps

Cut out simple designs from a foam sheet and use double-sided tape to attach them to a piece of thick cardstock or foam core. Use as you would a commercial stamp.

Punches

Punches are such fun. You can punch out patterns and motifs. Use the punched-out shapes to create your own motifs and to decorate cards, boxes, bags, and wrapping paper. A simple hole punch can be a useful tool, too.

DECORATIVE MATERIALS

Rivets and eyelets

These are great to use in card designs. You usually buy the rivets and eyelets in a kit along with a hole maker and a tool to hammer the reverse of the eyelets flat. These are obtainable from craft and dressmaking shops. You will need a hammer and a sturdy board to work on. I use a wooden breadboard and a lightweight hammer.

Wire

This comes in a variety of colors and thicknesses. Some outlets stock little pegboards that can be used for shaping wire. To cut wire, you will need a small pair of pliers or a pair of scissors kept specifically for this purpose.

Buttons and beads

An interesting bead or button can be the focus of a special card. I purchase them in thrift/secondhand stores, cut them off old clothes, and seek them out in fabric stores.

Braid, ribbon, and mesh

Ribbons, strings, threads, and yarns are useful for making handles on gift bags and as extra decoration on a card.

Gems

Faux gems add a little luxury to your cards. Use tiny gems as accents. Try craft stores for a selection of unusual stick-on gems.

Glitter

Glitter is useful when embellishing cards or making motifs. I prefer the finer glitters and occasionally use glittery embossing powder as glitter.

Oven-bake clay

Using this material is your chance to craft something unique. Try making small hearts, flowers, stars, and other shapes. Follow the manufacturer's instructions.

Transfers

There are a huge variety of designs available in many different styles—beautiful illustrations, comic characters, patterns, etc. Transfers are an extremely quick way to make an original card. Peel-offs are widely available and can be used on acetate or vellum and decorated with felt-tip pens to create stained glass effects.

Motifs, cutouts, and stickers

There is such a wide variety of motifs and cutouts available, you are bound to find something to suit your needs. Some are adhesive, others you will need to glue on. Look in cake decorating stores and stationery and craft shops.

CARD DESIGN

rafters are always on the lookout for new ideas. I keep a journal where I note down and sketch out ideas for all sorts of things, from greeting card designs to ideas for fundraiser sales, wedding cake designs, sketches of baby knits, or ideas for new recipes. Very often, something that I had intended for one project works for another. I tape in bits and pieces torn from magazines and inspirational photos taken on vacation. When I have a new project to create a design for, the first place I go to for inspiration is my journal. It is amazing how the roughest of sketches will remind me of a shirt I saw someone wearing when I was traveling on the Paris metro or a beach bag I noticed on a trip to the seaside. Simply make a record of anything that catches your "design" eye, as you never know when you might be able to use it.

I also have a large board where I pin up an ongoing collection of inspirational pictures and tear-outs. I position it so that I can see it from where I'm working, so my brain is always thinking of new ideas. When the board becomes overcrowded, I tape the most useful images into some sort of order in my journal.

I file away bits and pieces of paper and cardstock left over from design projects in themes and colorways. For example, scraps of Christmas gift wrap, brightly colored candy wrappers, Christmas stickers, used Christmas postage stamps torn from envelopes, and Christmas cards to be cut up and recycled get put in a file and labeled "Christmas." When the festive season is approaching, I sit down and go through the box, searching for inspiration. I also keep themed boxes for spring, flowers, new baby, and things suitable for children's cards. Having everything in one place is very useful, particularly when making homemade motifs.

Homemade motifs

I find commercially available motifs very useful and would not hesitate to use them. However, when I have the time, I try to make my own motifs. I find this very creative, as it gives me a chance to play with my materials when I am not under pressure to produce a card for a particular person or client. I save scraps left over from other projects and store them in a large box: my "motif" box. I keep punched-out shapes, interesting scraps of paper and cardstock, stickers, ribbons, buttons—basically, I don't throw anything away.

A few ideas as to the kinds of motifs that you can make are shown in the photograph opposite. Take the black cat motif, for example. One is made from a stamped image decorated with green gel pen eyes. The image is layered up on paper and cardstock, which outline and frame the picture. The other is a silver embossed cat, layered onto different-colored cardstock. You can use the same stamp, punch, sticker, or paper to create many different motifs. Change the color of the ink, cardstock, paper, or pen or cut the backing layers into different shapes and sizes.

Scoring and Folding

Scoring makes folding cardstock and paper easy and gives your finished cards a professional appearance. Use a stylus to score paper and cardstock. You should score on the outside of the card.

Hill and valley folds are basic origami folds and are useful to the card maker. I have used them in the Winter Wonderland card on page 186. A hill fold is scored on the front of the card and folded so that the fold peaks toward you. A valley fold is scored on the underside of the card so that the fold points away from you.

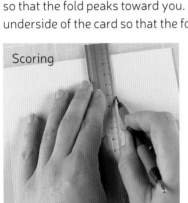

Scoring

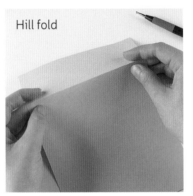

Hill fold

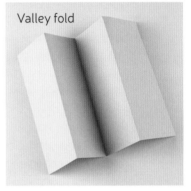

Valley fold

Tracing Templates

There are several ways of doing this, and you may already have your own way that you're happy with, so carry on! I like to trace patterns onto acetate using a marker, especially when I'm making templates for envelope inserts, gift pouches, bags, or really any pattern that I intend to use more than once. Obviously you can use tracing paper, but acetate is more robust and your templates will stay in good condition for longer.

DECORATING ENVELOPES

I'm not going to show you how to make envelopes, as they are available to buy in just about every size and color imaginable. I think it is more efficient to spend your time decorating envelopes to match your cards. Use stickers or motifs to decorate envelope covers. It is also fun to create inserts. You can use decorative paper, or line the envelope with tissue or mulberry paper and then use punches, stamps, gel pens, whatever you can think of to embellish the lining. Have fun and let your imagination run away with you.

Making an envelope lining

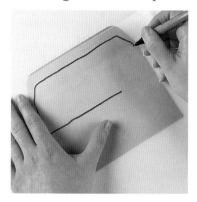

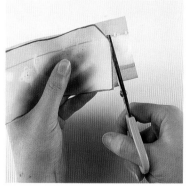

1 Select an envelope that you want to decorate and use it to create a template for the lining. Do this with acetate and a marker.

2 Use the template to cut out an insert from your chosen decorative paper.

3 Use spray adhesive (or double-sided tape) to attach the insert inside the envelope.

GIFT WRAP

aking gift wrap to coordinate with your cards is another way to use your design skills. It's your chance to create gorgeous wrapping papers, boxes, bags, and pouches that are much more desirable than anything you'll find in stores. You'll need to think about how you can take the design elements on the card and carry them through onto your additional materials. I often use the feature stencil, stamp, or theme of the card. For example, with Flower Power (page 92), simply sticking the punched flowers on paper looked good, while for Holly Berries (page 184), I made my own stamp. The foil decorated card Star Bright (page 188) looks great paired with embossed gold snowflake stamped tissue paper.

Take care to ensure that the shades of paper or cardstock you use are either the same as those on your card or complement the card. Also, remember to use the same embossing powders, paints, and pens. It is this attention to detail that will give your work a professional look.

Creating decorative gift wrap

The ways in which you can decorate gift wrap are almost limitless. Paper can be stamped, embossed, stenciled, decorated with punched shapes, covered in stickers—the list goes on and on. Look carefully at the card that you have made and decide how you can use part of the design on your gift wrap; then choose what paper to use as a base.

Tissue paper is my favorite wrapping medium, as it is a great background for all sorts of embellishment. It is widely available in a huge range of colors and shades, so you'll always find something suitable. I usually use two layers of tissue paper to wrap a gift—one is decorated and the other acts as plain backing. Use single sheets of decorated tissue to pad boxes containing delicate or small gifts, such as lingerie, baby clothes, or jewelry.

Brown paper printed or stenciled with gold or silver seasonal motifs makes great Christmas wrapping. White butcher's paper or lining paper looks great printed in primary colors—children's handprints or paint splatters look particularly interesting.

Pouches, bags, and boxes

Decorating commercially available gift bags, boxes, and pouches is quick and fun. They are available in all shapes, sizes, and colors, and you can add your own personal touches to them in a matter of minutes. Although it is nice to make your own bags and boxes, buying blanks is certainly the easiest option if you need to decorate 30 party bags or 100 wedding favors. However, even very plain gift bags can be expensive, so look out for other bags that you could use. Plain brown and white paper bags are cheap to buy and make great party bags. Recycle gift bags and boxes that are given to you. Everything that you buy these days seems to come with loads of packaging, so think about how you can reuse it.

If you need a bag of a particular size, you may need to make one yourself (see page 36 for instructions). If you need a large bag, make it from heavier paper. If this isn't possible, line the paper before you begin construction.

Gift pouches are the perfect alternative for hard-to-wrap presents.

BASIC GIFT POUCH

This simple gift pouch is easy to make and fun to decorate. Make pouches in different colors and decorate them to coordinate with your card or gift wrap.

Materials

+ Half letter/A5 sheet acetate
+ Marker
+ Craft knife
+ Cutting mat
+ Half letter/A5 sheet medium-weight cardstock
+ Low-tack masking tape
+ Scissors
+ Pencil
+ Stylus
+ Metal ruler
+ Eraser
+ Double-sided tape

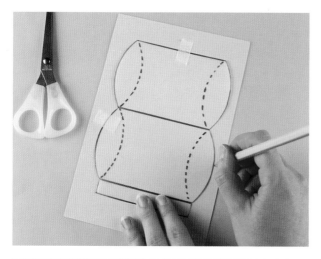

1 Trace the template on page 210 onto acetate using the marker. Cut out the template. Lay the template onto the sheet of cardstock and tack in position using low-tack masking tape. Draw around the template in pencil. Cut out the piece.

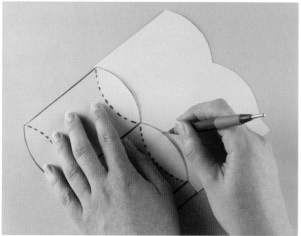

2 Use the stylus (and ruler when appropriate) to score the fold lines. Erase any visible pencil lines carefully before folding the scored lines.

3 Place a line of double-sided tape on the flap, fold over, and press down. Your pouch is now ready to decorate.

BASIC GIFT BAG

making a gift bag is simple. Use plain or patterned paper and make handles from string, rolled paper, or ribbon. The main thing to remember when making a gift bag is that the side folds should be the same depth as the bottom fold. Once you have mastered the technique, making bags will be quick and easy. Choose the size of your piece of paper to suit the gift that you want to put in the bag. You can punch holes in the top of the bag and thread ribbon through it or attach bought or homemade handles using white glue.

Materials
+ Sheet of paper
+ Double-sided tape
+ Scissors

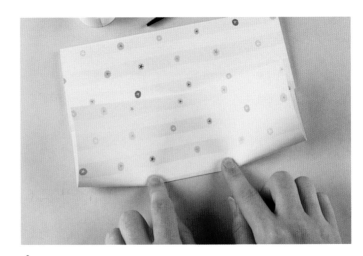

1 Take the side of the paper farthest away from you and fold it down toward the center. Then fold the side of the paper nearest to you up toward the center. Make sure that the ends overlap slightly. Use double-sided tape to secure down.

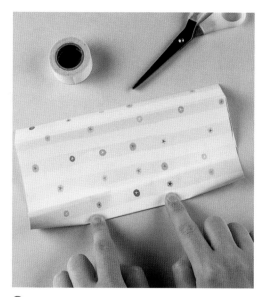

2 Fold the far side in ¾" (2cm). Press down on the fold firmly. Fold the near side in ¾" (2cm) and once again press down on the fold firmly.

3 Open out and push the folds that you have just made inward.

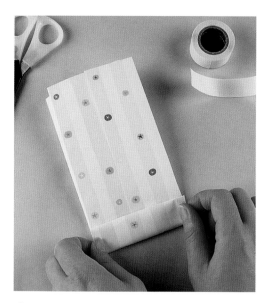

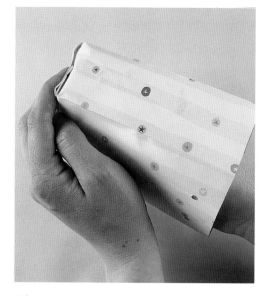

4 Place the folded bag on the surface in front of you. Fold the base of the bag up by ¾" (2cm). Press along the fold firmly. Make a second ¾" (2cm) fold upward and secure in place with double-sided tape.

5 Open up the bag by slipping your hand inside it and gently pressing out the corners.

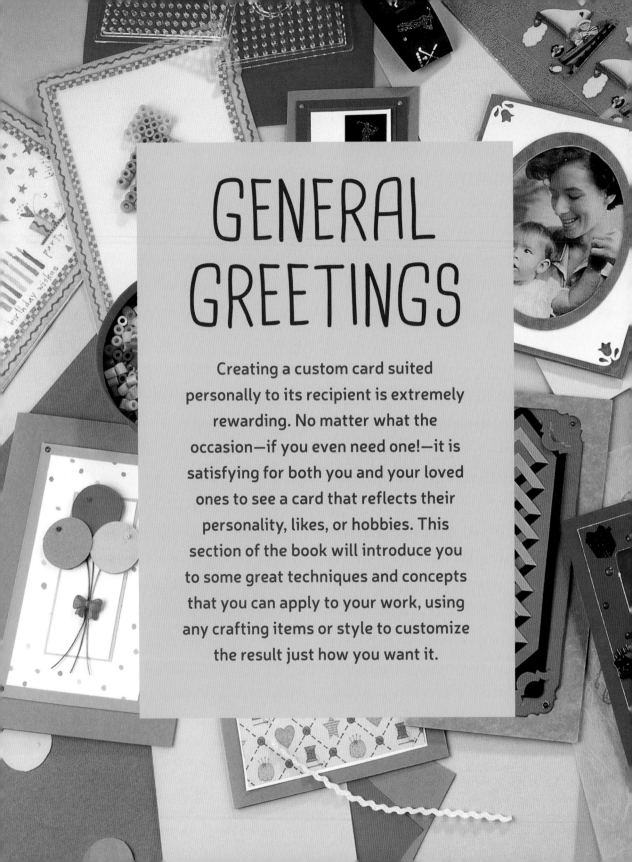

GENERAL GREETINGS

Creating a custom card suited personally to its recipient is extremely rewarding. No matter what the occasion—if you even need one!—it is satisfying for both you and your loved ones to see a card that reflects their personality, likes, or hobbies. This section of the book will introduce you to some great techniques and concepts that you can apply to your work, using any crafting items or style to customize the result just how you want it.

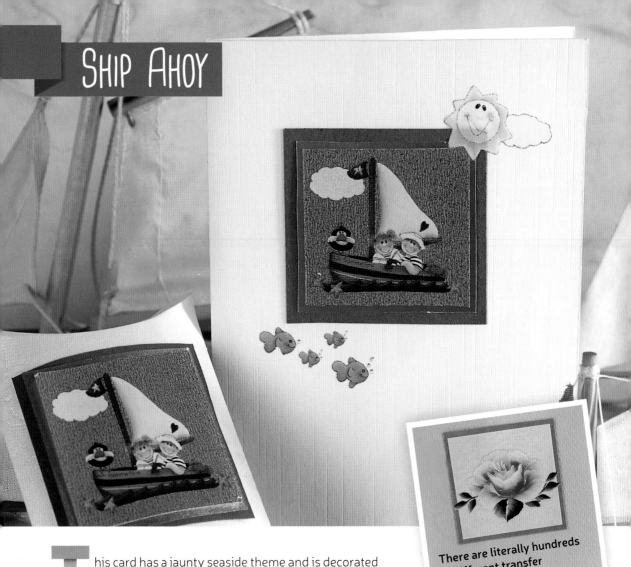

SHIP AHOY

There are literally hundreds of different transfer designs available.

T his card has a jaunty seaside theme and is decorated with rub-on transfers. Transfers are a quick and easy way to decorate gift pouches and gift bags as well.

Materials

- + Letter/A4 sheet white linen-finish cardstock
- + Stylus
- + Metal ruler
- + Blue cardstock
- + Silver cardstock
- + Blue glitter paper
- + Craft knife
- + Cutting mat
- + Pencil
- + Double-sided tape
- + Scissors
- + Rub-on transfer
- + Transfer stick

 Effort: Once the cardstock layers are cut to size, this card takes no time at all to make.

 Variation: Use a flower transfer on a white background, layer it onto coordinating paper, and attach to a pastel card base to create a Mother's Day card.

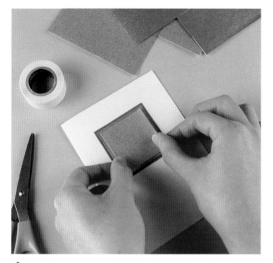

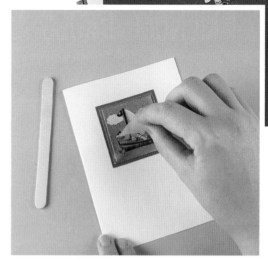

1 Score and fold the sheet of white cardstock to create the card base. To create the layers, cut a 2¼" (5.5cm) square from blue cardstock, a 2" (5cm) square from silver cardstock, and a 1¾" (4.5cm) square from blue glitter paper. Use double-sided tape to attach the squares in an upper central position on the card.

2 Cut around the transfer you wish to use, leaving a ¼" (0.5cm) border. Remove the backing sheet. Place the transfer on the blue glitter paper and use the transfer stick to rub over the image. Gently peel off the plastic sheet.

3 Cut out the accent decorations and transfer first the cloud and then the sun to the top right-hand corner. Transfer the fish on the left beneath the motif.

4 Finally, place a small transfer on the back of the card. This added extra gives your card a professional finish.

FRIENDLY FROGS

Cheeky frog stickers and 3D paint on brightly decorated card create a great child's birthday card or simply a cheering message to a friend.

Materials

- Letter/A5 sheet navy blue cardstock
- Metal ruler
- Stylus
- Half letter/A5 sheet yellow translucent paper
- Craft knife
- Cutting mat
- Pencil
- Spray adhesive
- Letter/A4 sheet white cardstock
- Double-sided tape
- Scissors
- Blue cardstock
- Yellow cardstock
- Black cardstock
- Green cardstock
- 3D tape
- Small frog stickers
- Green and blue 3D paint

Effort: Take your time when measuring and cutting the layers, as they are the focus of this card.

Variation: A row of robins on red, white, and brown cardstock layers would create a fun, seasonal card. For other animal-themed cards, try three sheep with shades of pastel green, white, and pink, or pink pigs on brown, white, and cream.

2 Attach the backed yellow paper centrally to the front of the card base with double-sided tape.

1 If using letter-sized dark blue cardstock, trim to 8½" x 5 ¹³⁄₁₆" (21.6 x 14.8cm) (A5). Score and fold to create the card base. Cut a 5" x 3½" (12.5 x 9cm) rectangle of yellow translucent paper. Spray it with spray adhesive and attach it to a piece of white cardstock to back it. Cut away the excess white cardstock.

3 Cut a 3" x 1½" (7.5 x 4cm) rectangle of blue cardstock and use double-sided tape to place it centrally on the yellow paper. Cut a 2½" x 1" (6 x 2.5cm) piece of yellow cardstock and layer this onto the blue cardstock.

4 Cut a 2¼" x ¾" (5.5 x 2cm) rectangle of white cardstock and tape it to the black cardstock. Cut a narrow frame. Tape the framed white cardstock to a piece of green cardstock and cut away all but a narrow frame.

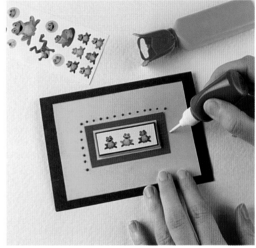

6 Starting with the frog in the middle, place three stickers on the white cardstock. Frame the motif with spots of blue 3D paint. Finally, squeeze a green spot of paint in each corner of the blue cardstock. If you have a spare sticker, attach it to the reverse of the card.

5 Create a 3D effect on the final layer of the card. Place three pieces of 3D tape on the back of the framed white cardstock and attach it to the central panel on the card.

INDIGO BLUE

Turn any of your snapshots into mini masterpieces. Here, the deep blue decorated paper complements the bark and green ivy in the photograph.

Materials

- Letter/A4 sheet white cardstock
- Craft knife
- Metal ruler
- Cutting mat
- Pencil
- Spray adhesive
- Sheet indigo blue decorative paper
- Photograph of suitable size
- Double-sided tape
- Scissors
- Dark blue cardstock

Effort: Once you have chosen your image, this card is super quick to make.

Variation: You could use any photograph in this way—perhaps shots of trips or family occasions. For a good result, it is important to spend time choosing the paper that will frame your image.

1 Cut the sheet of white A4 cardstock in half (to create two A5 pieces), or, if using US letter paper, cut a piece that is 8½" x 5 ¹³⁄₁₆" (21.6 x 14.8cm) (A5). Score and fold this piece to create the card base and set the other piece aside for now. Spray a layer of spray adhesive on the exterior of the card base. Lay it on the sheet of decorative paper and cut away the excess paper with a craft knife.

2 Draw a 2½" x 1½" (6 x 4cm) rectangle around an area of your chosen photograph and cut it out.

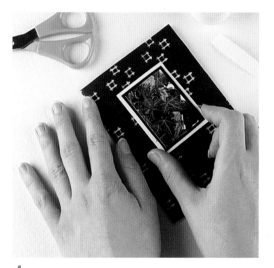

3 Use double-sided tape to attach the photograph to a small piece of dark blue cardstock. Use scissors to cut away all but a ¼" (0.5cm) frame.

4 Use double-sided tape to attach the framed photograph to a small piece of white cardstock and once again cut away all but a ¼" (0.5cm) frame. Attach the layered motif in an upper central position on the front of the card.

HOW DOES YOUR GARDEN GROW?

Flowers and seed beads are used to good effect in this earthy card. This card is a perfect greeting for a friend who spends all of his or her free time in the garden.

Materials

- Letter/A5 sheet of speckled buff cardstock
- Metal ruler
- Stylus
- Rectangle cutter, template, and board
- White cardstock
- Scissors
- Pencil
- Green cardstock
- Craft knife

- Cutting mat
- Double-sided tape
- Blue translucent paper
- Spray adhesive
- Sheet scrap paper
- Brown and silver mix seed beads
- Plants, watering can, and garden tools cutouts

Effort: While away a pleasant half-hour making this card for a gardening friend.

Variation: Try a snow scene using white accent beads on a blue background decorated with dark cutout branches and a tiny robin sticker.

1 If using letter-sized speckled buff cardstock, trim to 8½" x 5 ¹³⁄₁₆" (21.6 x 14.8cm) (A5). Score and fold to create the card base. Use the rectangle cutter to cut a 1½" x 3" (3.75 x 7.5cm) rectangular window from white cardstock. Cut a narrow border around the window.

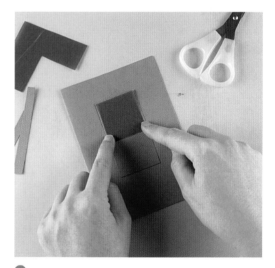

2 Cut out a 1¾" x 3¼" (4.25 x 8cm) rectangle of green cardstock. Use double-sided tape to attach it in an upper central position on the card front. Measure and cut out a 1¾" x 1½" (4.5 x 4cm) piece of blue translucent paper. Use spray adhesive to attach it to the upper half of the green cardstock.

4 Use double-sided tape to attach the white frame on top of the green and blue rectangle. The garden is now ready for planting with flowers and foliage.

3 Place a strip of double-sided tape to cover a little of the blue and a little of the green cardstock. Fold a sheet of scrap paper in half and open it out. Put the card onto the scrap paper and sprinkle accent beads over the tape. Do this gently, as these little beads roll everywhere! Shake the card to remove any loose beads and return them to the pot.

5 Press the watering can, flowers, and tools cutouts in place. If you are unable to buy prepared cutouts, make your own from scraps of paper and cardstock using the templates on page 211.

Pastimes

Hobbies and pastimes make good starting points when designing a card for a friend or relative.

Materials

- Half letter/A5 sheet olive green cardstock
- Metal ruler
- Pencil
- Craft knife
- Cutting mat
- Stylus
- Half letter/A5 sheet dark red cardstock
- Double-sided tape
- Scissors
- Half letter/A5 sheet dark green cardstock
- Half letter/A5 sheet cream cardstock
- Patterned ribbon
- Small piece black cardstock
- Golf shoes and club (cake/scrapbooking decorations)
- Super glue
- Hole punch
- White glue
- Small piece white cardstock
- Gold 3D paint
- Flower sticker

 Effort: This card is extremely quick to make.

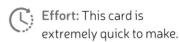 **Variation:** Both craft and cake decorating stores stock a wide variety of hobby-related decorative items, so you can create many different cards using this design concept as a base.

1 Cut out a 5½" x 5¼" (13.5 x 14cm) rectangle of olive green cardstock. Score and fold in half to create the card base.

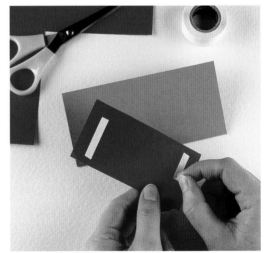

2 Cut out a 4¼" x 2¼" (10.5 x 5.5cm) rectangle of dark red cardstock. Use double-sided tape to attach it in an upper central position on the front of the card.

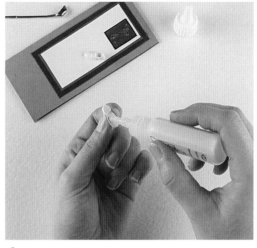

4 Your card is now ready to decorate. Cut a piece of patterned ribbon so that the motif is in the center, and use double-sided tape to attach to a piece of black cardstock. Cut away all but a narrow frame around the ribbon. Tape it in the upper right-hand corner of the cream cardstock. Use super glue to secure the golf shoes and club in place.

3 Take the dark green cardstock and cut out a 3¾" x 1¾" (9.5 x 4.5cm) rectangle. Use double-sided tape to attach it centrally on the dark red cardstock. Measure and cut out a 3½" x 1½" (9 x 4cm) rectangle from cream cardstock. Use double-sided tape to attach it on top of the dark green cardstock.

5 Punch three small circles out of white cardstock and use white glue to stick them in a row beneath the framed picture. Paint a gold 3D dot in the corners of the dark red cardstock. Put the flower sticker in the bottom right-hand corner.

SEW SIMPLE

Make this design in other colorways, using interesting buttons as a central feature.

Buttons, lace, and themed paper create the perfect card for a friend who's handy with a needle.

Materials

+ Letter/A4 sheet blue cardstock
+ Craft knife
+ Cutting mat
+ Metal ruler
+ Pencil
+ Stylus
+ Decorative paper
+ Double-sided tape
+ Scissors
+ Half letter/A5 sheet white cardstock
+ Green translucent paper
+ White rickrack
+ 3 blue buttons

Effort: A quick card suitable for birthday greetings or a thank-you note.

Variation: Themed paper is easy to find in craft shops. A sheet of romantically decorated paper and a framed row of pretty pearl buttons would make a lovely wedding card.

1 Cut the sheet of blue A4 cardstock in half (to create two A5 pieces), or, if using US letter paper, cut a piece that is 8½" x 5 ¹³⁄₁₆" (21.6 x 14.8cm) (A5). Score and fold this piece to create the card base and set the other piece aside for now. Cut out a 3½" x 5" (8.5 x 12.5cm) rectangle from the decorative paper. Use double-sided tape to attach it to the white cardstock. Cut away all but a thin frame around the paper. Use double-sided tape to attach the framed item centrally on the card front.

2 Cut a ¾" x 2" (2 x 5cm) piece of white cardstock. Use double-sided tape to attach this to a piece of blue cardstock. Cut away all but a narrow frame. Next, layer this up on green translucent paper using double-sided tape. Cut a narrow frame around the blue cardstock.

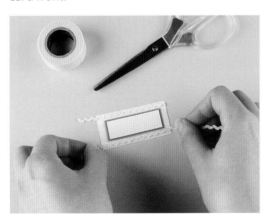

3 Use double-sided tape to attach the layered design to white cardstock. Cut a ¼" (0.5cm) frame around it. Place thin strips of double-sided tape on the white frame. Lay and press the rickrack down on the tape to secure it firmly. Trim the rickrack as needed. Layer up onto blue cardstock and cut a ¼" (0.5cm) border.

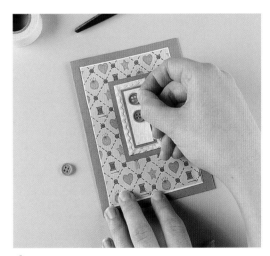

4 Use double-sided tape to attach the framed item centrally on the card front. Tape the buttons onto the cardstock layers. You might want to add a little decoration to the back of the card, too. Try using a motif cut from the decorative paper.

The design for this versatile card was inspired by the ornately decorated wrapping paper. Use the paper to decorate tags, pouches, and boxes.

Materials

- + Letter/A4 sheet of cream cardstock
- + Craft knife
- + Pencil
- + Metal ruler
- + Triangle/set square
- + Cutting mat
- + Stylus
- + Embossing stamp pad

- + Rubber stamp
- + Sheet of scrap paper
- + Gold embossing powder
- + Tweezers or tongs
- + Precision heat tool
- + Patterned wrapping paper
- + Double-sided tape
- + Scissors
- + Gold paper

Effort: Take your time measuring and folding to ensure a stylish finish. Refer to page 30 for more information on folding.

Variation: All you need to do to create a totally different card is to choose another stamp and different wrapping paper.

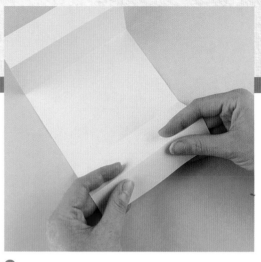

2 Using the triangle/set square and stylus, make hill folds at 1" (3cm) and 9" (23cm) and valley folds at 3" (8cm) and 7" (18cm).

1 Cut a 5" x 10" (13 x 26cm) rectangle out of the cream cardstock. Make small, light pencil marks at 1" (3cm), 3" (8cm), 7" (18cm), and 9" (23cm). These indicate where the folds will be.

3 Open up the card and, using the embossing stamp pad, stamp the shape in a central position on the open card base. Place the stamped card onto a sheet of scrap paper. Sprinkle with the gold embossing powder. You need to do this before the ink dries.

4 Shake the excess powder onto the scrap paper and return the excess to the container. Holding the stamped card with tweezers or tongs, heat the powdered design with the precision heat tool until glossy and set.

5 The card is now ready for decoration. Cut two 1" x 5" (2.5 x 13cm) pieces of patterned paper. Use double-sided tape to attach the pieces to the open edges of the card. Cut two more pieces of patterned paper, this time 2" x 5" (5 x 13cm) each, and attach to the reverse fold with double-sided tape.

6 Cut two 4" (10cm) strips of gold paper. One should be ¼" (0.5cm) wide and the other ⅛" (0.25cm) wide. Attach them to the inside of the card, one above the other, approximately ¾" (2cm) from the bottom of the card.

lean whites and shimmery gold give this card an air of sophisticated understatement. Use this card as a party or wedding invitation, to say thank you, or to send birthday greetings.

Materials

- Letter/A5 sheet cream textured cardstock
- Stylus
- Metal ruler
- Craft knife
- Cutting mat
- Pencil
- Embossing pad
- Peacock feather stamp

- Sheet plain white cardstock
- Scrap paper
- Gold embossing powder
- Precision heat tool
- Double-sided tape
- Scissors
- Sheet shimmery gold cardstock
- Sheet pale yellow parchment
- Gold 3D paint

Effort: Stamped cards are quick and easy to make, and therefore are quite suitable for mass production.

Variation: Use a poppy stamp and emboss it in brilliant red and green to create a different, but still very stylish, card.

Create a decorative frame using a corner cutter, and then mount a wonderfully colored feather in it.

2 Fold a sheet of scrap paper in half. Hold the stamped white cardstock over the paper and sprinkle with gold embossing powder. Shake off the excess powder and return it to the container.

1 Trim the cream textured cardstock to 7½" x 5 ¹³⁄₁₆" (19 x 14.8cm). Score and fold to create the card base. Using the embossing stamp pad, print a single peacock feather on a sheet of plain white cardstock.

3 Use the precision heat tool to set the embossed design.

4 Once the paper has cooled, measure a 4" x 2" (10.5 x 5cm) rectangle around the embossed design so that it is in the center. Cut out.

6 Attach the framed design to a sheet of pale yellow parchment. Cut away all but a ½" (1cm) frame. Attach with double-sided tape to the card front and decorate with four gold 3D paint dots, one in each corner of the parchment frame.

5 Use double-sided tape to attach the design to a piece of gold cardstock. Cut away all but a narrow frame of gold.

BEAD DOLLY

These cards were created by my children. Use beads to create simple designs and geometric patterns. You can make a card suitable for any occasion.

Fusible beads and pegboards have been a part of my life for as many years as I have had children. They can be used to create both simple and intricate designs.

Materials

+ Letter/A5 sheet of plastic sheeting or vellum
+ Stylus
+ Metal ruler
+ Letter/A5 sheet white paper
+ Double-sided tape
+ Scissors
+ Patterned paper napkin
+ Spray adhesive
+ Red, flesh, blue, and yellow fusible beads and pegboard
+ Iron

 Effort: Bead art takes time and patience, so have fun creating your own designs.

 Variation: A bead Christmas decoration would look good on a plastic sheeting base with a seasonal edging cut from a Christmas napkin. Make the decoration removable so that it can be used on the tree for years to come

1 If using letter-sized plastic sheeting and white paper, trim both to 8½" x 5 ¹³⁄₁₆" (21.6 x 14.8cm) (A5). Score and fold both pieces in half and attach the white paper inside the plastic sheeting using double-sided tape.

2 Cut out the border pattern from the paper napkin. Separate the patterned layer from the backing layers.

3 Use spray adhesive to attach the napkin border around the edge of the plastic sheeting cover. Cut away any excess and be sure to miter the corners (cut them at an angle) for a perfect fit.

4 Use the pattern on page 211 to make the dolly design using fusible beads and the pegboard. Fuse the beads using an iron, following the manufacturer's instructions. Use double-sided tape to attach the bead dolly centrally on the card.

The dove of peace flies across a glittering sky holding an olive branch. For an alternative design, create a sunny, rainbow-filled sky.

Materials

- Oval cutter, template, and board
- Half letter/A5 sheet blue cardstock
- Scrap paper
- Spray adhesive
- Chunky glitter
- Half letter/A5 sheet olive green cardstock
- Letter/A5 sheet white textured cardstock
- Double-sided tape
- Scissors
- Acetate
- Fine-tip black pen
- White cardstock scrap
- Spring green cardstock scrap
- White glue

Effort: This card takes a little time, as you need to take care when cutting out the various elements.

Variation: A red card base and gold oval could frame a winter backdrop featuring a chubby snowman with a carrot nose.

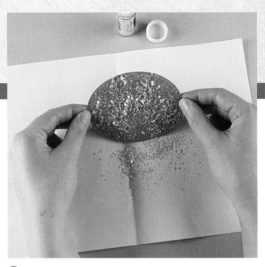

2 Fold a sheet of scrap paper in half and open it up. Coat the blue oval with spray adhesive and, holding it over the scrap paper, sprinkle it with chunky glitter. Shake off the excess glitter and return it to the container.

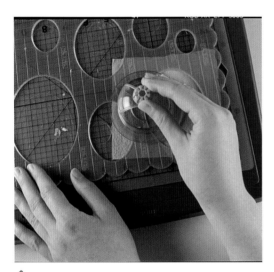

1 Use the oval cutter, template, and board to cut out a 4" x 3" (10 x 7.5cm) oval in blue cardstock. If you do not have an oval cutter, use the template on page 212.

3 Using the oval cutter, cut a 4" x 3" (10 x 7.5cm) oval from olive green cardstock. Now cut a second, slightly smaller oval from the center of the first. You now have a frame. If you do not have an oval cutter, use the template on page 212.

4 If using letter-sized white textured cardstock, trim to 8½" x 5 ¹³⁄₁₆" (21.6 x 14.8cm) (A5). Score and fold to create the card base. Use double-sided tape to attach the blue oval in a central position on the front of the card. Tape the green frame directly on top of the blue oval.

5 Trace the dove and olive branch templates on page 213. Cut the dove pieces out of white cardstock and the olive branch from spring green cardstock. Use white glue to attach the bird in a central position within the frame. First place a wing, then the body, and finally the second wing.

6 Use a black fine-tip pen to draw around the edge of the bird's body and wings and to draw an eye. Use white glue to attach the olive branch so it looks as though the bird is carrying it in its beak.

This card contains both a gift and a greeting. The bookmark can be removed and will be a wonderful reminder of a birthday or special occasion.

Materials

- + Pattern-cutting sheet
- + Cutting mat
- + Masking tape
- + Scissors
- + Mauve and pink two-tone paper
- + Craft knife
- + Metal ruler
- + White glue
- + Double-sided tape
- + Black cardstock
- + Mauve cardstock
- + Corner cutter
- + Purple ink dauber (or dauber with purple paint/inkpad)
- + Mottled gray cardstock
- + Stylus
- + Silver 3D paint
- + 4 green seed beads

Effort: Take your time when marking and cutting the pattern for this card; it has to be precise.

Variation: You could make a bookmark using an embossed, stamped design. Make up a base in coordinating colors.

2 Fold the cutout chevrons to create the pattern and use white glue to hold them in place. Shape the top and bottom into points. Use double-sided tape to attach the chevron pattern centrally on a 5¼" x 1⅞" (13.5 x 4.75cm) rectangle of black cardstock. Shape the top of the black cardstock into a point and round all the corners.

1 Secure the cutting sheet to a cutting mat with masking tape. Slide a 5¼" x 1½" (13 x 4cm) piece of two-tone paper under the chevron pattern and cut a line of chevrons 3½" (8.5cm) long. (If you do not have a pattern-cutting sheet, use the template on page 213. Trace onto acetate, then cut through the marked chevrons to create the folding areas.)

3 Cut out a 5½" x 2½" (14 x 6cm) piece of mauve cardstock. Use a corner cutter to cut out each corner. You must make cuts that are spaced to hold the bookmark in place.

4 Press a purple ink dauber around the edge of the mauve cardstock.

6 Slip the bookmark in place. Put tiny dots of silver 3D paint in each corner of the mauve bookmark holder. Place a bead on each paint dot.

5 Cut out a 6½" x 6¼" (16.5 x 16cm) piece of mottled gray cardstock. Score and fold it in half to create the card base. Use double-sided tape to attach the bookmark holder centrally on the card base.

MEMORIES

W hen searching for an idea for a Mother's Day card, I came across this long-forgotten photograph. I hope it inspires you to make something similar for someone special in your life.

Materials

- Letter/A4 sheet mottled brown cardstock
- Craft knife
- Metal ruler
- Pencil
- Cutting mat
- Stylus
- Oval cutter, template, and board

- Half letter/A5 sheet textured cream cardstock
- Photograph
- Corner punch
- Double-sided tape
- Scissors
- Half letter/A5 sheet cream paper

Effort: Take your time when making this card; it's a gift as well as a greeting.

Variation: Try the card in more modern colors if you are using a recent, color photograph.

1 Cut an 8¼" x 5" (21 x 13cm) rectangle from the sheet of mottled brown cardstock. Score and fold it in half to create the card base. Use the oval cutter, template, and board to cut your photograph into a 4" x 3" (10 x 7.5cm) oval shape. If you do not have an oval cutter, use the templates on page 214.

2 Cut a 4" x 4¾" (10 x 12cm) rectangle out of textured cream cardstock. Cut a 3½" x 2½" (9 x 6.5cm) oval in a central position on the cream cardstock. Cut a 4¼" x 3" (10.5 x 7.5cm) oval from mottled brown cardstock and then cut a 3½" x 2½" (9 x 6.5cm) oval out of that. This will frame the photograph.

4 Use double-sided tape to layer up the card. Tape the photograph in position beneath the decorated cream cardstock and attach the frame. Attach the completed picture to the card front.

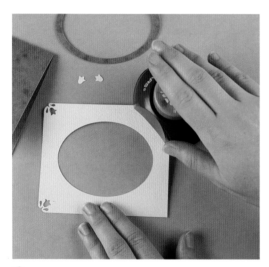

3 Use a punch to decorate each corner of the cream cardstock. (If you do not have a corner punch, try trimming the cardstock with scissors and decorating it with dots of 3D paint).

5 Cut an 8" x 4¼" (20 x 11cm) rectangle from cream paper. Fold it in half and affix in place inside the card with double-sided tape.

ELEPHANT TRAILS

A wealth of history and craftsmanship has gone into creating this card. The stamp is one of many commercially available stamps handcrafted in India using traditional skills, local wood, and hand tools.

Materials

- Letter/A4 sheet white cardstock
- Craft knife
- Metal ruler
- Cutting mat
- Stylus
- Spray adhesive
- Embroidered paper
- Elephant stamp
- Red stamp pad
- Scrap paper
- Red sparkle embossing powder
- Tweezers or tongs
- Precision heat tool
- Pencil
- Gold pen
- Cardstock in green, yellow, blue, red, and gold
- Double-sided tape
- Scissors
- 3D double-sided tape

 Effort: Take your time stamping and embossing the feature design.

Variation: Traditional wooden stamps come in all shapes and sizes. Enjoy creating your own designs with handmade stamps.

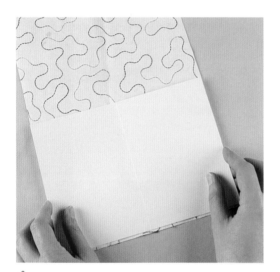

1 Cut the sheet of white A4 cardstock in half (to create two A5 pieces), or, if using US letter paper, cut a piece that is 8½" x 5 ¹³⁄₁₆" (21.6 x 14.8cm) (A5). Score and fold this piece to create the card base and set the other piece aside for now. Spray a layer of spray adhesive on the exterior of the card base and set it aside for a minute or two to become tacky. Then lay the card base onto the reverse side of the embroidered paper. Smooth into place and cut away any excess.

2 Using your chosen stamp and the red stamp pad, print a selection of images across the white cardstock. Fold a sheet of scrap paper in half and open it out. Place the white cardstock on the scrap paper and sprinkle the embossing powder over the images. Shake off the excess powder and return it to the pot.

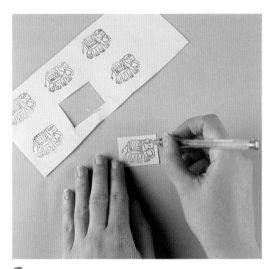

4 Cut out the layers: a 2½" x 2"
(6.25 x 5.25cm) rectangle of red
cardstock; a 2¼" x 1¾" (5.5 x 4.5cm)
rectangle of blue cardstock; a 2" x 1½"
(5 x 4cm) rectangle of yellow cardstock; and
a 1¾" x 1¼" (4.5 x 3.5cm) rectangle of green
cardstock. Use double-sided tape to attach
them one on top of the other (in the order in
which you cut them out) on the card base.

3 Holding the stamped cardstock with
tweezers or tongs, seal the embossing
powder with the precision heat tool. Select
the best image and use the ruler and pencil
to mark up a 1½" x 1¼" (4 x 3cm) rectangle
around it. Cut it out. Highlight the image with
the gold pen.

**A sheet of beautifully crafted wrapping
paper can be used to make a gift bag or
to cover a gift pouch (see pages
34–37).**

5 Use double-sided tape to attach the
stamped and embossed elephant to a
piece of gold cardstock. Cut a narrow border
around the image. Use 3D double-sided tape
to attach it to the layers.

No collection of cards is complete without a pop-up design. This card would make a great birthday greeting for a young friend.

Materials

+ Letter/A4 sheet red cardstock
+ Craft knife
+ Metal ruler
+ Cutting mat
+ Pencil
+ Stylus
+ Rectangle cutter, template, and board
+ Half letter/A5 sheet blue shimmer cardstock
+ Double-sided tape
+ Scissors
+ Birthday cake and present sequins
+ Red 3D paint
+ Glow-in-the-dark star
+ Silver pen
+ Sheet of plastic sheeting or vellum

Effort: Take your time over this card, as it is important to get the construction right.

Variation: Once you have mastered the art of the pop-up, the sky's the limit. Use different background colors and replace the star with a flower, spaceship, bee, birthday cake, or anything you want!

2 Cut out a 2½" x 4" (6 x 10cm) rectangle from the center of the sheet of blue shimmer cardstock. Cut a ½" (1.25cm) border around the rectangular hole to create a frame. Use double-sided tape to attach it to the front of the card to frame the window.

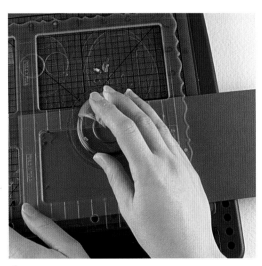

1 Cut the sheet of red cardstock in half lengthwise. Take one piece and score and fold it in half to create the card base. Cut out a 2½" x 4" (6 x 10cm) rectangle from the front of the card base.

3 Use double-sided tape to attach birthday cake and present sequins around the frame.

4 Use red 3D paint to print a pattern of dots between the sequins. Leave to dry.

6 When the paint is dry, assemble the card. Cut a ¼" x 5½" (0.5 x 14cm) strip of plastic sheeting. Tape one end to the interior of the card and attach the star to the other end.

5 Tape the glow-in-the-dark star to a piece of red cardstock. Cut around it to leave a frame. Decorate the frame using a silver pen, and embellish the star with red 3D paint.

Balloon Magic

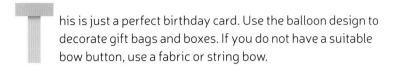This is just a perfect birthday card. Use the balloon design to decorate gift bags and boxes. If you do not have a suitable bow button, use a fabric or string bow.

Materials

- + Letter/A5 sheet of violet cardstock
- + Stylus
- + Ruler
- + Half letter/A5 sheet green cardstock
- + Craft knife
- + Cutting mat
- + Pencil
- + Double-sided tape
- + Scissors
- + Sheet polka dot paper
- + White cardstock scrap
- + Yellow cardstock scrap
- + Blue, red, and yellow craft wire
- + Super glue
- + Circle cutter, template, and board
- + Blue and red cardstock scraps
- + 3D tape
- + Bow-shaped button
- + 3 seed beads—blue, red, and yellow
- + Purple 3D paint

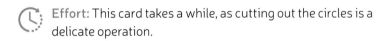**Effort:** This card takes a while, as cutting out the circles is a delicate operation.

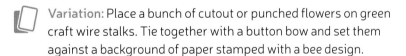**Variation:** Place a bunch of cutout or punched flowers on green craft wire stalks. Tie together with a button bow and set them against a background of paper stamped with a bee design.

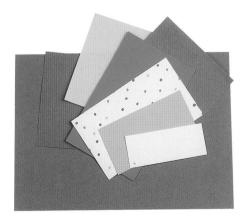

2 Cut a 1¼" x 3" (3 x 7.5cm) rectangle out of white cardstock. Attach it to a piece of yellow cardstock and cut away all but a narrow frame of yellow. Attach these layers centrally on the polka-dot paper.

1 If using letter-sized violet cardstock, trim to 8½" x 5 ¹³⁄₁₆" (21.6 x 14.8cm) (A5). Score and fold to create the card base. Cut a 4¾" x 3" (12 x 7.5cm) piece of green cardstock. Use double-sided tape to attach it centrally on the card base. Cut a 4½" x 2½" (11 x 6.5cm) piece of polka-dot paper. Tape this to the green cardstock.

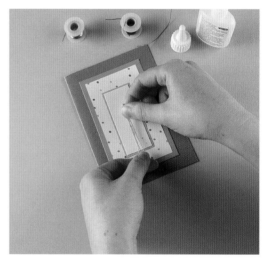

3 Cut 2¾" (7cm) of blue, red, and yellow wire. Use super glue to attach a short section of the bunch of wire "strings" to the card. Allow to dry. Fan out the top and bottom of the wires.

4 Use the circle cutter, template, and board to cut two 1" (2.5cm) circles from blue, red, and yellow cardstock.

6 Use super glue to attach the bow and the beads. Paint purple 3D dots at each corner of the green cardstock.

5 Using double-sided tape, position the bottom layer of each balloon circle on the card to correspond with the matching color wire. Place the circles underneath the wires. Put 3D tape on top of the wires, then put the top layers of the balloons in place.

KALEIDOSCOPE

eople have been folding paper to create patterns for generations. Teabag folding is an intricate system to create kaleidoscope-like effects.

Materials

+ Half letter/A5 sheet blue cardstock
+ Craft knife
+ Metal ruler
+ Pencil
+ Cutting mat
+ Stylus
+ Half letter/A5 sheet white cardstock
+ Double-sided tape
+ Scissors
+ Half letter/A5 sheet orange cardstock
+ Sheet of decorative paper (suitable for folding)

 Effort: You should spend some time practicing your paper folding.

 Variation: The pattern created will depend on the colors of the paper squares you use.

1 Cut an 8¼" x 4" (21 x 10cm) rectangle out of the blue cardstock. Score and fold in half to create the card base. Cut a 2¾" (7cm) square piece of white cardstock. Use double-sided tape to attach it to the orange cardstock. Cut away all but a narrow orange frame around the white cardstock. Use double-sided tape to attach this piece to the card front.

2 Cut four 2" (5cm) squares of decorative paper. Place a square of decorated paper face up on a flat surface. Fold in half in both directions. Open it up, then fold in half diagonally in both directions. Push in the sides to form a triangle.

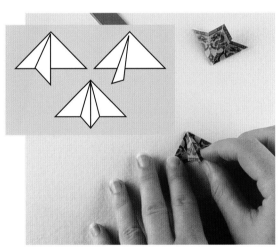

3 Fold one corner toward the central fold line. Fold the corner back on itself. Make the same fold on the other side of the triangle. Open out both folds and flatten them to make the final shape. Repeat the entire folding process with the other three squares.

4 Use double-sided tape to attach the four folded shapes to the card.

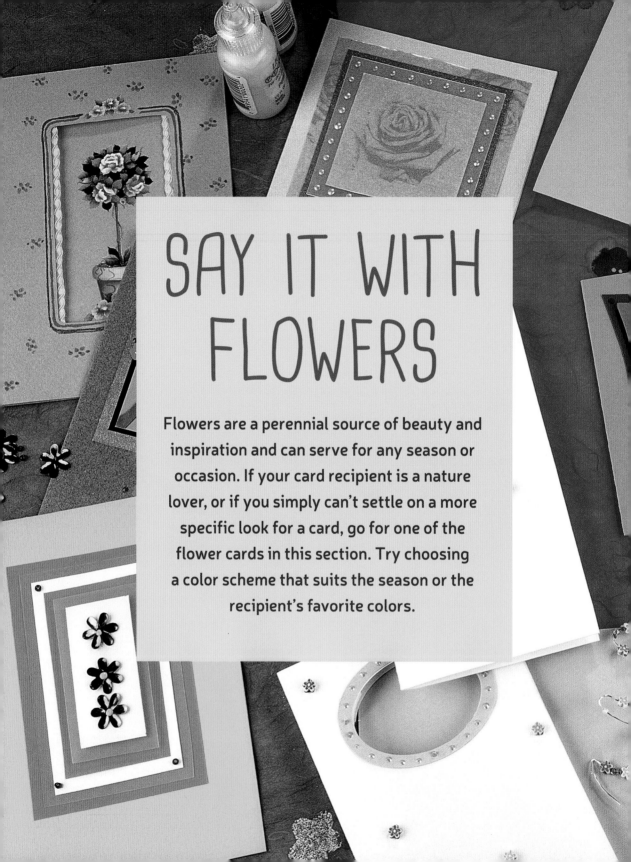

SAY IT WITH FLOWERS

Flowers are a perennial source of beauty and inspiration and can serve for any season or occasion. If your card recipient is a nature lover, or if you simply can't settle on a more specific look for a card, go for one of the flower cards in this section. Try choosing a color scheme that suits the season or the recipient's favorite colors.

FLOWER POWER

This display of paper flowers strewn across a violet card will bring a little summer magic into someone's life.

Materials

+ Letter/A5 sheet violet cardstock
+ Metal ruler
+ Stylus
+ Craft knife
+ Cutting mat
+ Pencil
+ Large flower punch
+ Small flower punch
+ Yellow, pink, red, orange, green, and blue construction (sugar) paper
+ Tweezers
+ White glue
+ Pale green gel pen
+ Yellow 3D paint

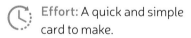

Vary the background color and try your hand at decorating a gift box or tag using punched paper flowers. Use a flower stamp to decorate tissue paper. You might want to use embossing powder to highlight the flower petals or centers.

Effort: A quick and simple card to make.

Variation: Decorate a sky blue card with punched butterflies. Replace the gel pen dots with tiny stamped daisies.

1 If using letter-sized violet cardstock, trim to 8½" x 5 ¹³⁄₁₆" (21.6 x 14.8cm) (A5). Score and fold to create the card base. Use the metal ruler and craft knife to trim the folded card to a height of 4½" (11cm).

2 Use the punches to cut out a selection of large and small flowers from construction (sugar) paper. Use white glue to attach small flowers centrally on large flowers.

3 Attach the prepared flowers across the card in an attractive pattern using white glue.

4 Use the pale green gel pen to draw small dots between the flowers. Finally, decorate each flower with a centrally placed dot of yellow 3D paint.

Gingham and daisies come together to create this delightfully pretty card. Cover gift boxes with daisy-stamped gingham paper and make coordinating gift tags.

Materials

- Letter/A5 sheet white cardstock
- Metal ruler
- Stylus
- Spray adhesive
- Pink gingham paper
- Craft knife
- Cutting mat
- Small piece white cardstock
- Pencil
- Four small flower rubber stamps
- Pink stamp pad
- Sheet of scrap paper
- Pink embossing powder
- Precision heat tool
- Double-sided tape
- Scissors
- Small piece dark pink cardstock
- Pink 3D paint

Effort: This card is easy to make, but take care when using the embossing powder. Make sure that you cover your work surface with scrap paper.

Variation: Try this design in blue or green gingham with a stamped flower feature. Or how about red gingham with red hearts?

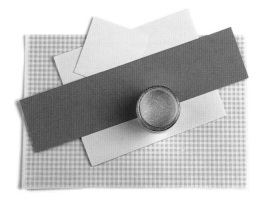

2 Cut a piece of white cardstock measuring 2¼" (5.5cm) square. Using the rubber stamps and a pink inkpad, stamp four different flowers onto the square.

1 If using letter-sized white cardstock, trim to 8½" x 5 ¹³⁄₁₆" (21.6 x 14.8cm) (A5). Score and fold to create the card base. Spray spray adhesive over the exterior of the card. Lay the gingham paper onto the sticky card base and smooth it down, removing any air bubbles. Trim away any excess.

3 Fold a sheet of scrap paper in half and open out. Holding the printed white square over the paper, sprinkle pink embossing powder over it. Shake off the excess powder and return it to the pot.

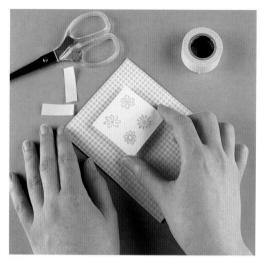

4 Seal the embossing powder with the precision heat tool. Use double-sided tape to attach the prepared flower picture in an upper central position on the front of the card.

6 Place four pink 3D paint dots, one in each corner of the frame, to give the card a professional finished look.

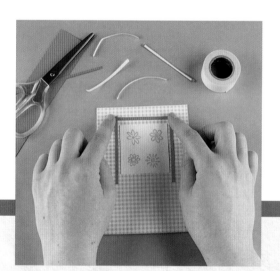

5 Cut out four narrow 3¼" (8cm) strips from the dark pink cardstock. Use double-sided tape to attach them to the card to create a frame. The strips should overlap.

Paper Roses

Use tissue paper to make unusual gift bag handles: Spray a thin layer of spray adhesive across a sheet of tissue paper, then crinkle and roll the paper, pressing to make a length of "rope."

A s soon as I saw this lovely gift wrap, I had loads of great ideas for using it to make beautiful cards, bags, and tags.

Materials

+ Half letter/A5 sheet purple cardstock
+ Craft knife
+ Cutting mat
+ Metal ruler
+ Pencil
+ Stylus
+ Rose-patterned wrapping paper
+ Double-sided tape
+ Scissors
+ Silver cardstock
+ Sheet of plastic sheeting or vellum
+ Purple 3D paint

 Effort: This card can be made in a matter of minutes, making it ideal to mass-produce for wedding invitations or thank-you notes.

 Variation: Gift wrap with a nautical theme would be fun to use here. Cut out a picture of a ship and set it against a blue backdrop.

1 Cut the card base out of the purple cardstock. It should measure 8¼" x 4" (21 x 10cm). Score and fold in half. Cut a 3½" x 3¼" (8.75 x 8.5cm) rectangle from the wrapping paper. Attach it in a central position on the card base using double-sided tape.

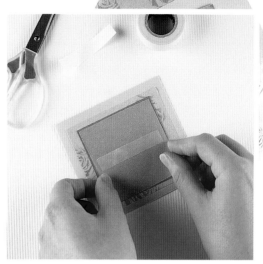

2 Cut out a 3" x 2⅞" (7.5 x 7.25cm) piece of silver cardstock. Use double-sided tape to attach it in a central position on the rose-patterned square. Cut a 2¾" x 2⅝" (7 x 6.75cm) piece of plastic sheeting and adhere this on top of the silver cardstock.

3 Draw a 2¼" x 2" (5.5 x 5.25cm) box around a rose on the patterned paper. Cut out. Use double-sided tape to attach it centrally on the plastic sheeting.

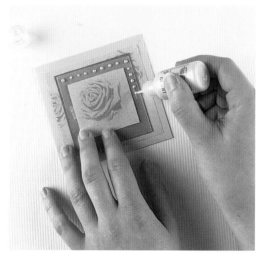

4 Use purple 3D paint to place dots around the edge of the plastic sheeting to frame the rose.

DAISY RAINBOW

 rainbow of daisies decorates this bright yellow card, with highlights in green and gold.

Have fun with your daisy punch. Use it to create wrapping paper, gift tags, boxes, and pouches.

Materials

+ Half letter/A5 sheet yellow cardstock
+ Craft knife
+ Cutting mat
+ Metal ruler
+ Stylus
+ Gold and green pens

+ Daisy punch
+ Blue, red, pink, and white paper
+ White glue
+ Tweezers
+ Purple 3D paint

Effort: This card is very impressive, yet extremely easy to make. Using a punch is a quick way of working.

Variation: A line of randomly placed punched dragonflies set against a dark blue base would make a stunning card.

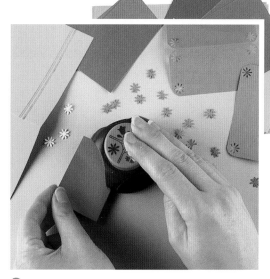

1 Cut an 8¼" x 4" (21 x 10cm) rectangle from the yellow cardstock. Score and fold to create the card base. Open it out. Use a ruler and the green and gold pens to draw lines down the card, front and back.

2 Punch about 20 daisies out of the colored papers.

3 Place dots of white glue on and around the ruled lines. Position the daisies on the glue dots.

4 Squeeze a dot of purple 3D paint in the center of each flower and also groups of dots between the flowers.

Green Blossoms

Hot orange tones and bright green blossoms decorate this versatile card.

Materials

+ Letter/A5 sheet bright yellow textured cardstock
+ Metal ruler
+ Stylus
+ Half letter/A5 sheet white cardstock
+ Craft knife
+ Cutting mat
+ Sheet of vellum
+ Double-sided tape
+ Scissors
+ 3 green flower sequins
+ Half letter/A5 sheet orange cardstock
+ 3D tape
+ Yellow 3D paint
+ White glue
+ 4 green seed bead

Effort: Flower sequins are quick and easy to use.

Variation: Pretty buttons set against layers of paper and cardstock would be an interesting option.

Experiment with colors and produce your own designs using flower sequins.

2 Turn the white cardstock and vellum piece vellum side up and use double-sided tape to attach three green flower sequins along the length of the white cardstock.

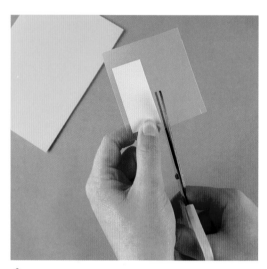

1 If using letter-sized yellow cardstock, trim to 8½" x 5 ¹³⁄₁₆" (21.6 x 14.8cm) (A5). Score and fold to create the card base. Cut a 1" x 2¼" (2.5 x 5.5cm) piece of white cardstock. Use double-sided tape to attach it to a vellum sheet. Use scissors to cut away all but a narrow frame around the white cardstock.

3 Attach the sequin piece to a small piece of orange cardstock using 3D tape. Cut away all but a ¹⁄₁₆" (0.4cm) edge around the sequin piece's vellum edge.

4 Use double-sided tape to attach the layers you have just assembled to white cardstock. Cut away all but a ⅛" (0.5cm) frame of white cardstock. Then attach this to another vellum sheet and cut a ⅛" (0.5cm) border of vellum around the white cardstock.

6 Put a yellow 3D paint dot in the center of each flower. Use white glue to attach a green seed bead in each corner of the white cardstock.

5 Use double-sided tape to attach the multi-layered piece to the orange cardstock and cut away one more frame of ⅟₁₆" (0.4cm). Finally, adhere the layered, framed piece in an upper central position on the front of the card using double-sided tape.

Funky Foam Flowers

This stylish card is made from foam sheets that come in a wonderful array of colors and are easy to shape, cut, and stick.

Materials

+ Letter/A4 sheet spring green cardstock
+ Pencil
+ Craft knife
+ Cutting mat
+ Metal ruler
+ Stylus
+ Scrap paper
+ Scissors
+ Half letter/A5 sheet blue cardstock
+ Green, blue, pink, and purple foam sheets
+ Double-sided tape
+ Pink and purple 3D paint

Effort: This card takes a little time to make, as you need to cut the foam carefully.

Variation: Make a Valentine's card with red, white, and hot pink layers decorated with red hearts. Embellish with silver 3D paint.

1 Cut an 8½" x 4¼" (22 x 11cm) rectangle from the sheet of green cardstock. Score and fold to create the card base. Trace and cut out the templates on pages 215–216. Draw around the largest square shape onto the blue cardstock and cut the shape out.

2 Cut the medium square out of green foam and the small square out of blue foam. Cut out two large flowers from pink foam, one large and one small flower from purple foam, and three leaves from green foam.

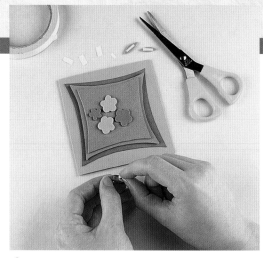

3 Take the green card base and, using double-sided tape, attach the blue cardstock layer, followed by the green foam layer and the blue foam layer.

4 Use double-sided tape to attach the flower and leaf shapes. Refer to the photograph for their positioning.

Cut out a selection of flowers and leaves from the foam sheets and use them to decorate gift boxes and cards. You might want to try the design in a different color scheme.

5 Decorate the card with 3D paint using pink on the purple flowers and purple on the pink flowers, as well as the corners of the blue cardstock.

TOPIARY

se rub-on transfers to create this lovely country garden scene. Once you have made the card, try decorating a gift box or pouch using the same motif.

Materials

- + Letter/A5 sheet pink cardstock
- + Metal ruler
- + Stylus
- + Rectangle cutter, template, and board
- + Lacy pattern vellum paper
- + Scissors
- + Double-sided tape
- + Garden motif rub-on transfers
- + Transfer stick
- + Green, pink, and violet gel pens

Effort: Putting together the elements of this card takes a little time, but the finished result will bring a great deal of pleasure to the recipient.

Variation: Window cards are very impressive. Use an interesting stamp—detailing the color with felt-tip pens—in place of the transfer.

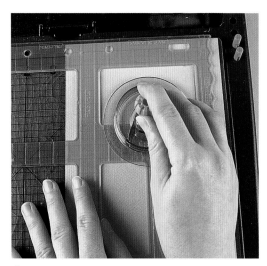

1 If using letter-sized pink cardstock, trim to 8½" x 5 ¹³⁄₁₆" (21.6 x 14.8cm) (A5). Score and fold to create the card base. Use the shape cutter, template, and board to cut out a centrally placed 2" x 3½" (5 x 9cm) rectangle on the card front.

2 Cut two 4" (10cm) strips of vellum. Use double-sided tape to attach the strips to the interior of the card on either side of the window to give it a thin, lace border.

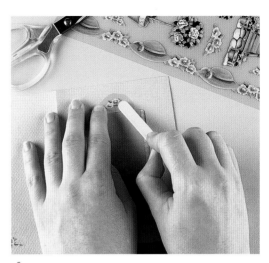

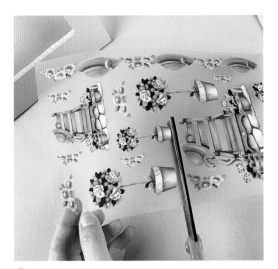

3 Cut out a suitable transfer and, following the manufacturer's instructions, transfer the design onto the interior of the card. The motif should be placed centrally so that it can be seen through the window.

4 Apply a second transfer to the front of the card, placing it centrally above the window. Use a third transfer to decorate the back of the card.

5 Frame the window with two borders using the green and pink gel pens. These can be drawn using a ruler or freehand. Complete the card by drawing little flower buds all across the front using the gel pens.

CHERRY BLOSSOM

Flower punches are so versatile. I use them all the time. This blossom-covered card was inspired by pictures of spring.

Materials

- Letter/A5 sheet gray cardstock
- Metal ruler
- Stylus
- Scissors
- Pencil
- Half letter/A5 sheet silver cardstock
- Half letter/A5 sheet black cardstock
- Half letter/A5 sheet turquoise blue cardstock
- Double-sided tape
- Small flower punch
- Pink paper
- Marker
- Small piece of acetate
- Small piece brown cardstock
- White glue
- Tweezers
- Silver and green 3D paints

 Effort: Set aside an hour to make this card, as there are a number of elements to prepare.

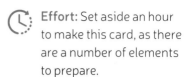 **Variation:** Use this technique to create a Christmas card. Use a brightly colored base and a silver frame; attach Christmas decorations to the branch.

1 If using letter-sized gray cardstock, trim to 8½" x 13⁄16" (21.6 x 14.8cm) (A5). Score and fold to create the card base. Cut out a 3¼" (8cm) square from silver cardstock, a 2¾" (7cm) square from black cardstock, and a 2½" (6.5cm) square from turquoise blue cardstock. Use double-sided tape to attach the silver square in a high central position, then adhere the black and blue squares on top.

2 Your card is ready to decorate. Punch out about 22 flowers from the pink paper.

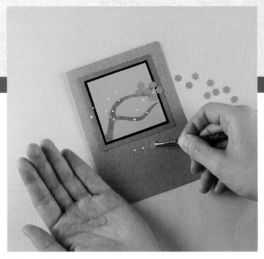

3 Use the marker to trace the branch template on page 217 onto acetate. Cut the shape out of brown cardstock and attach it to the front of the card using double-sided tape. The branch should look as though it is growing out of the bottom left-hand corner of the blue square.

4 Squeeze 22 dots of white glue where the flowers will be placed. Cherry blossom grows in clusters of three or four blooms, so bear this in mind. Place a flower on each glue dot. Glue three flowers in a row beneath the picture.

This card base is gold and black gift wrap, and the flowers punched from gold paper are set against black. Use gold gel pen to draw on stems and leaves.

5 Place dots of green 3D paint between the flowers to resemble leaves (three or four leaves per cluster of flowers). Squeeze a dot of silver 3D paint in the center of each flower. Don't forget to dot leaves and flower centers on the flowers beneath the picture.

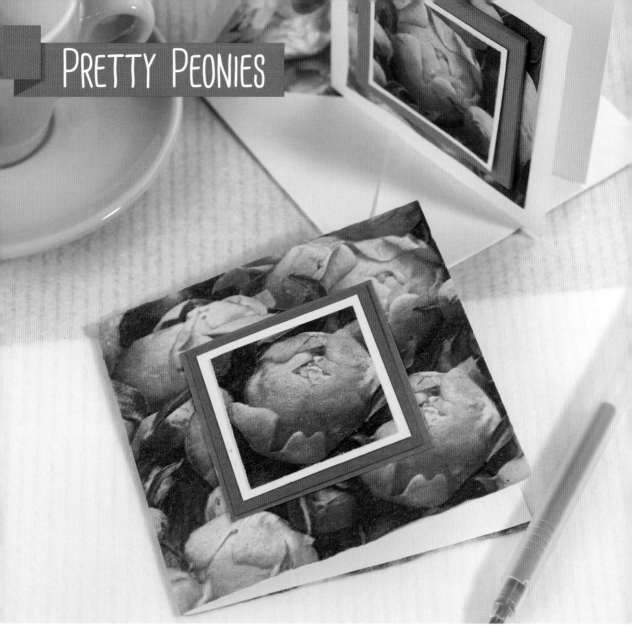

Pretty Peonies

When I found these beautifully decorated paper napkins, I just had to have them. Paper napkins decorated with flowers are so inspirational, and pictures of peonies or roses make the most romantic greeting cards.

Materials

- + 2 decorative paper napkins
- + Letter/A4 sheet white cardstock
- + Craft knife
- + Metal ruler
- + Cutting mat
- + Stylus
- + Spray adhesive
- + Letter/A4 white paper
- + Pencil
- + Small piece green cardstock
- + Small piece red cardstock
- + Small piece white cardstock
- + Double-sided tape

Effort: Once you have mastered the method, this card is quick and simple to create, making it a good design for mass production.

Variation: Make this card in yellow and white daisies for a country feel.

Use the peony napkins as gift wrap and to decorate boxes and tags.

1 Take the table napkins and separate the patterned layer from the remaining tissue layers. You will use the patterned layer to decorate your card. Discard the other layers.

2 Cut out an 8¼" x 4" (21 x 10cm) rectangle from white cardstock. Score and fold to make the card base. Spray the card base with spray adhesive and position it on the back of the patterned tissue layer. Turn over and carefully smooth the tissue onto the card base. Trim away the excess tissue.

3 Spray the letter/A4 sheet of white paper with spray adhesive. Smooth the second patterned tissue layer over it to attach firmly.

4 Take the decorated paper sheet and use a pencil and ruler to mark up a 1¾" (4.5cm) square for the central motif. Cut out with a craft knife.

5 Cut a 2½" (6cm) square from green cardstock, a 2¼" (5.5cm) square from red cardstock, and a 2" (5cm) square from white cardstock. Use double-sided tape to attach the central motif square centrally on the white square.

6 Layer this piece onto the red square and then finally the green square. Use double-sided tape to attach the layered design centrally on the card.

irework and flower beads are framed in mint green and white to create this pretty card. Use bead and wire designs to coordinate bags and gift tags.

Materials

- + Letter/A4 sheet of white line-embossed cardstock
- + Craft knife
- + Metal ruler
- + Cutting mat
- + Stylus
- + Pencil
- + Rectangle cutter, template, and board
- + Small piece pale green cardstock
- + Double-sided tape
- + Selection of pastel colored beads
- + Silver wire
- + Wire cutters
- + White glue
- + Pink 3D paint

Effort: Threading and gluing the bead design for this card takes a little while.

Variation: To create a Christmas card, make a red frame and thread the wire with silver and clear beads and tiny stars. Scatter stars across the front of the card.

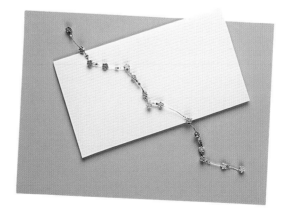

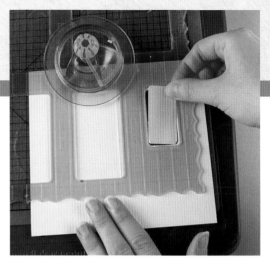

2 Using the point you have just marked as a guide, cut a 2" x 1" (5 x 2.5cm) window from the front of the card using the rectangle cutter.

1 Cut a 6¼" x 6" (16 x 15cm) rectangle from the white cardstock. Score and fold to make the card base. Make a mark at the horizontal center of the card front, about one third of the way down.

3 Cut the same-sized window from green cardstock. Measure a ⅛" (0.5cm) border around the window and cut out.

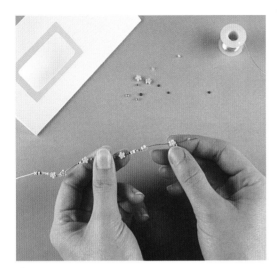

4 Use double-sided tape to attach the green frame around the window in the front of the card. Thread beads onto an 8¼" (21cm) length of silver wire. Pinch the ends of the wire over so that the beads do not fall off as you work.

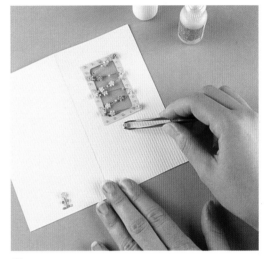

6 Mark dots in pink 3D paint along the frame. Use white glue to attach a single bead ⅛" (0.5cm) below the window.

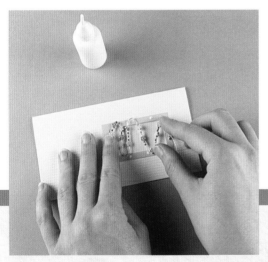

5 Shape the beaded wire into 1½" (3.5cm) zigzags. Use white glue to attach it to the card.

SPECIAL OCCASIONS

Our lives are full of special days, moments, and events that are worthy of celebration. You can make a card for any of these occasions, and show your loved ones how much you truly care. Whether you're making a card for a birthday, a new baby, or a marriage, there will be something in this section to inspire you.

Patchwork House

Construct a gift bag using suitable wrapping paper. Decorate it with a fabric collage to coordinate with your card, along with a gift tag.

This heartwarming little card is made from scraps of floral patchwork fabric. It's a perfect way to wish friends good luck in their new home.

Materials

+ Half letter/A5 sheet pale pink textured cardstock
+ Metal ruler
+ Craft knife
+ Cutting mat
+ Pencil
+ Stylus
+ Tracing paper
+ 4 scraps of patchwork fabric
+ Scissors
+ Spray adhesive
+ Green gel pen
+ Pink 3D paint

Effort: Once you've gathered together the scraps of fabric, this card is quick to make.

Variation: Try a fabric collage in bright modern colors for a more stylish look. You could even try a paper collage.

1 Measure and cut out a 6¼" x 4¾" (16 x 12cm) rectangle from the pink cardstock. Score and fold in half to create the card base.

2 Trace the house template on page 217 and cut out the various shapes from your chosen fabrics.

3 Use spray adhesive to attach the fabric pieces on the card to form the house. The house should be in a lower central position.

4 Add details to the windows and door using the green gel pen. Complete the card by painting five pink 3D paint dots coming out of the chimney.

SILVER STREAMERS

C raft gems look great on cards. Here I have combined faux diamonds with silver thread and red hearts to create a modern yet romantic look, perfect for Valentine's Day or an anniversary.

Materials

- Red oven-bake clay
- Mini rolling pin
- Board
- Plastic wrap
- Heart cutter
- Baking tray
- Stylus
- Ruler
- Letter/A5 sheet white textured cardstock
- Double-sided tape
- Scissors
- Silver thread
- Half letter/A5 white paper
- Super glue
- Tweezers
- Faux diamond

 Effort: This card is very easy to make, but you will need to set aside a little time to bake the clay hearts.

 Variation: Tiny stars and a faux jewel would create a stunning card to send best wishes to someone, or even for a Christmas greeting.

1 Soften a small piece of red oven-bake clay and roll out between two layers of plastic wrap. Cut out a dozen or so tiny red hearts and bake according to the manufacturer's instructions. (Don't forget to remove the plastic wrap.)

2 If using letter-sized white cardstock, trim to 8½" x 5 ¹³⁄₁₆" (21.6 x 14.8cm) (A5). Score and fold to create the card base. Place three strips of double-sided tape horizontally on the inside of the card front—one at the top, one in the middle, and one at the bottom.

4 Cut an insert of white paper that is slightly smaller than the card and attach it to the inside of the card with double-sided tape.

3 Wind silver thread around the front panel of the card, making sure it has a firm grip on the double-sided tape. Check the silver thread pattern you are creating on the front as you go.

5 Use super glue to attach the red hearts to the card. Use double-sided tape to stick the faux diamond in place.

SPARKLING HEARTS

This romantic card is perfect for sending Christmas wishes to a loved one. These glittery hearts would look good on gift wrap and tags, too.

1 Cut a 6¾" x 7" (17 x 18cm) shape from the cream paper. Score and fold in half to make the card base. Tear a 6½" x 2¾" (16.5 x 7cm) rectangle from the red paper. Use double-sided tape to attach it in a central position to the card front.

2 Cut a 6" x 2½" (15 x 6cm) rectangle from the white textured cardstock. Attach it in a central position on the red paper with double-sided tape.

4 Trace the template on page 217. Use it to cut three heart shapes from the red paper. Use a glue stick to attach them to the red glitter paper. Cut around each heart shape, leaving a narrow border of red glitter paper.

3 Tear out three 1¾" x 2" (4.5 x 5cm) pieces of white line-embossed paper. Edge the torn pieces with gold glitter glue and set aside to dry.

5 Glue the hearts onto the gold-edged torn white paper pieces to create the motifs. Using double-sided tape, attach the central heart motif to the card, then position the other two hearts.

BUNCH OF HEARTS

irework can be very stunning. I have framed the wire design here with tissue paper. Decorate bright pink tissue paper with gold dots to make gift wrap and use the card design to make gift tags.

Materials

- + Half letter/A5 sheet cream textured cardstock
- + Metal ruler
- + Craft knife
- + Cutting mat
- + Stylus
- + Pink tissue paper
- + Spray adhesive
- + Yellow paper

- + Blue paper
- + Double-sided tape
- + Scissors
- + Red, yellow, blue, and pink craft wire
- + Wooden dowel
- + Super glue
- + Gold 3D paint

Effort: This card takes a little time to make, but it is well worth the effort.

Variation: Cut snowflakes out of tissue paper. Use spray adhesive to attach them to a card base, then embellish with 3D paint.

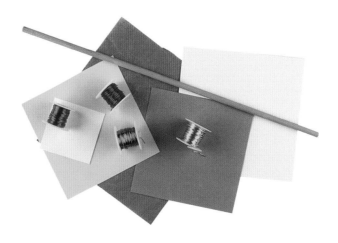

2 Using double-sided tape, cut and assemble the layers for the central motif in this order: a 2¼" (5.5cm) square of yellow paper, a 2" (5cm) square of blue paper, and a 1¾" (4.5cm) square of cream cardstock. Attach the layers centrally on the pink square.

1 Use a craft knife to cut a 4" x 8¼" (10.5 x 21cm) rectangle from the cream cardstock. Score and fold to form the card base. Tear a piece of bright pink tissue paper about 3½" (8.5cm) square. Use spray adhesive to attach it in a central position on the front of the card.

3 Wind a length of red wire around a dowel three times and then stretch out a 4" (10cm) length. Cut off. Slide the wire off the dowel and press the coils together.

4 Measure 1¼" (3cm) up from the coils and make a circle of wire ½" (1cm) in diameter. Wind the excess wire around the stem. Press the top of the circle down in to create a heart shape. Trim excess wire. Make hearts in blue and yellow wire as well. Use super glue to attach the hearts on the cream cardstock.

6 Use gold 3D paint to outline and decorate the pink tissue paper. You could put a pink tissue paper or wire heart on the back of the card for an extra touch.

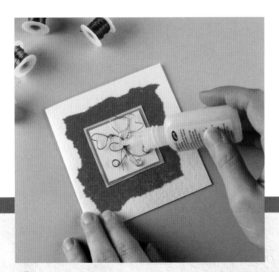

5 Cut a 2½" (6cm) length of pink wire. Make two loops, then twist into a bow shape. Trim and affix into position with super glue.

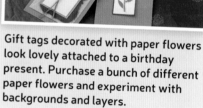

Gift tags decorated with paper flowers look lovely attached to a birthday present. Purchase a bunch of different paper flowers and experiment with backgrounds and layers.

A sheet of angel hair paper and a bunch of red paper rosebuds were used to create this beautiful card. To create a wonderful birthday card, use pink roses and pink paper instead.

Materials

+ Letter/A5 sheet pink cardstock
+ Metal ruler
+ Stylus
+ Sheet white translucent paper
+ Sheet angel hair paper
+ Craft knife
+ Cutting mat

+ Double-sided tape
+ Scissors
+ Sheet red handmade paper
+ Small piece green cardstock
+ Small piece white cardstock
+ 2 paper rosebuds
+ Gold yarn
+ White glue
+ 2 red heart sequins

 Effort: Once the shapes are cut out, this card takes no time to make at all.

 Variation: To make a simple but unique card, attach a small bunch of silk lily of the valley to a sage green card base.

1 If using letter-sized pink cardstock, trim to 8½" x 5 13⁄16" (21.6 x 14.8cm) (A5). Score and fold to create the card base. Measure and cut out 4¼" x 2¼" (10.5 x 5.5cm) rectangles of white translucent and angel hair paper. Use double-sided tape to attach the white translucent paper in a central position on the card base. Adhere the angel hair paper on top.

2 Tear a 3¼" x 1¾" (8 x 4.5cm) rectangle from the red handmade paper. Cut a 2¾" x 1½" (7 x 3.5cm) rectangle from the green cardstock and a 2½" x 1¼" (6.5 x 3cm) rectangle from the white cardstock. Using double-sided tape, layer the red paper, the green cardstock, and finally the white cardstock onto the angel hair paper.

3 Tie the two rosebud stems together with a 4" (10cm) length of gold yarn. Use white glue to attach firmly in place on the card.

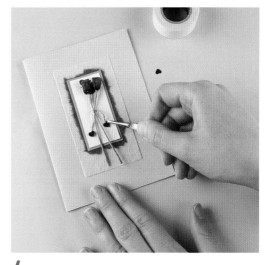

4 Trim the ends of the yarn to about ¾" (2cm) in length. Use double-sided tape to attach the red heart sequins to the ends of the yarn.

WEDDING CAKE

This is a true confection in candy pink, crisp white, and subtle silver with which you can send wedding greetings. Use the cake motif to decorate boxes and pouches. These could also be used for wedding favors.

Materials

- Letter/A4 sheet white textured cardstock
- Craft knife
- Metal ruler
- Cutting mat
- Stylus
- Half letter/A5 sheet pink cardstock
- Double-sided tape
- Scissors
- Sheet of plastic sheeting or vellum
- Silver and white 3D paint
- Acetate
- Marker
- Pink gel pen
- Silver pen
- Silver cardstock
- Silver wire
- Pencil
- Silver heart sequin
- White glue
- Hole punch
- Thin white ribbon

Effort: The sophisticated simplicity of this card takes a little while to achieve.

Variation: Make this card in lemon yellow and replace the cake with a silver stork sticker to make a delightful newborn baby card.

1 Cut out a 6½" x 6" (16 x 15cm) piece of white textured cardstock. Score and fold in half to create the card base. Measure and cut out a 5½" x 2½" (14 x 6cm) rectangle from the pink cardstock. Use double-sided tape to attach it in a central position on the card base.

2 Cut a rectangle of plastic sheeting measuring 2¼" x 5" (5.5 x 12.5cm). Use double-sided tape to attach it to the card front in a central position. Ensure that the tape is centrally placed on the plastic sheeting so it will remain invisible on the finished card. Place a silver 3D paint spot in each corner of the plastic sheeting.

3 Trace the templates on page 218 onto acetate using marker. Cut the pieces out of white textured cardstock. Draw a pink scallop pattern along the upper edges of the cake layers. Use silver pen to color in the cake boards along the lower edges of the cake layers.

4 Cut four narrow ½" (1cm) ribbons of silver cardstock. These will make the cake stands. Cut two 3¼" (8cm) lengths of silver wire. Make a curl in the end of each length of wire by wrapping them around a pencil.

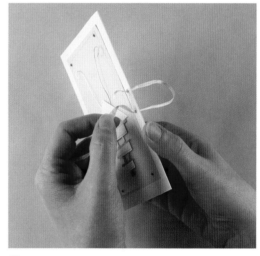

6 Use a hole punch to make two holes on the left side of the card. Thread white ribbon through the holes and tie a bow.

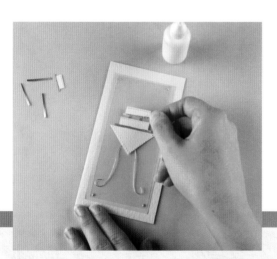

5 Use double-sided tape to assemble the card. Begin by laying the wire table legs in place. Attach the remaining pieces from the bottom up. Glue the heart sequin in place at the top and decorate the tablecloth with a border of white 3D dots if desired (visible in this step photo).

Pretty cake ribbon is used to decorate this wedding card. Visit your local cake decorating store; you'll find plenty to inspire your greeting card creativity.

The mulberry paper used for this card makes a great base for a variety of cards and tags. The double hearts shown here were purchased from a cake decorating shop.

Materials

+ Letter/A4 sheet white cardstock
+ Stylus
+ Metal ruler
+ Craft knife
+ Cutting mat
+ Spray adhesive
+ White heart-decorated mulberry paper

+ Half letter/ A5 sheet gold cardstock
+ Double-sided tape
+ Scissors
+ Decorative ribbon 2" (5cm) wide

Effort: This card is easy to make and can be quickly mass-produced, making it an ideal wedding invitation.

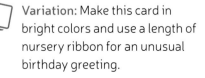

Variation: Make this card in bright colors and use a length of nursery ribbon for an unusual birthday greeting.

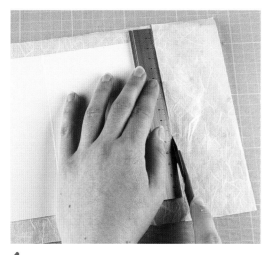

1 Cut the sheet of white A4 cardstock in half (to create two A5 pieces), or, if using US letter paper, cut a piece that is 8½" x 5 ¹³⁄₁₆" (21.6 x 14.8cm) (A5). Score and fold this piece to create the card base and set the other piece aside for now. Apply spray adhesive on the outside of the card base. Lay this on top of the mulberry paper. Smooth the paper over the card and use a craft knife to cut away the excess from around the card base.

2 Cut a 4" x 2½" (10 x 6cm) piece of gold cardstock and a 3¾" x 2¼" (9.5 x 5.5cm) piece of white cardstock. Use double-sided tape to layer them centrally on the card base.

3 Measure and cut a 3½" (9cm) length of ribbon. Be sure to cut it so that the image is in the center of the piece of ribbon.

4 Use spray adhesive to attach the ribbon centrally on the white cardstock, creating a framed picture.

Tiny Onesie

I love this card. To me it is everything a new arrival card should be—simple, pretty, and unbelievably cute.

Materials

- Small piece white textured cardstock
- Deckle-edge scissors (decorative paper edger)
- Pencil
- Metal ruler
- Blue and yellow 3D paint
- Cutout of baby outfit
- Acetate
- Marker
- Blue foam sheet scrap
- Scissors

- Small length of gold craft wire
- Double-sided tape
- 3D tape
- Letter/A5 sheet baby blue cardstock
- Half letter/A5 sheet white cardstock
- Half letter/A5 sheet blue gingham paper
- Half letter/A5 sheet yellow cardstock
- Large and small flower punches
- White glue

 Effort: Set aside a quiet hour to make this special greeting card.

Variation: Three-dimensional cards are very impressive. Cutouts that represent a hobby or interest would look good when used in this way.

1 Use the deckle-edge scissors to cut a 2" x 3" (5 x 7.5cm) rectangle from the sheet of white textured cardstock. Edge with a line of blue 3D paint. Leave to dry.

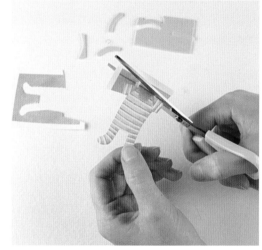

2 Cut out a baby outfit and back it if necessary. Trace the coat hanger template on page 218 using the marker. Construct the hanger using the foam sheet and wire. Use double-sided tape to attach it to the sheet of blue-edged cardstock. Use 3D tape to attach the baby outfit on top, giving the impression that it is hanging up.

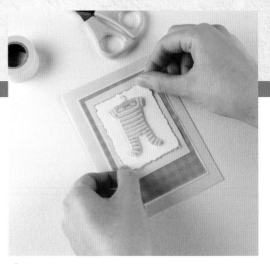

3 If using letter-sized baby blue cardstock, trim to 8½" x 5 ¹³⁄₁₆" (21.6 x 14.8cm) (A5). Score and fold to create the card base. Cut a 5" x 3¼" (12.5 x 8cm) rectangle of white cardstock and a 4¾" x 3" (12 x 7.5cm) rectangle of gingham paper. Attach the gingham paper to the white cardstock using spray adhesive, then attach the white cardstock to the card base in a central position using double-sided tape.

4 Cut out a 3½" x 2½" (9 x 6.5cm) rectangle of yellow cardstock. Use double-sided tape to attach it in an upper central position on the gingham paper. Finally, adhere the baby outfit motif on top of that.

This design works well in pink as well as blue. You can make an array of items to match the card, including gift bags, tags, and lined envelopes (see page 31).

5 Punch out one large and two small flowers from the white cardstock. Use 3D tape to stick the large flower underneath the motif. Glue the two small flowers on either side of it. Dot yellow 3D paint centers on each flower and in the corners of the framed picture.

ROCKING HORSE

his framed rocking horse makes a lovely card. It would be wonderful to use for baby announcement cards or thank-you notes for new baby gifts.

Materials

- Letter/A5 sheet white textured cardstock
- Metal ruler
- Stylus
- Sheet pink cardstock
- Craft knife
- Cutting mat
- Double-sided tape
- Sheet white cardstock
- Sheet silver cardstock
- Peel-off sticker
- Embossing board and heart template
- Pink 3D paint

 Effort: Peel-offs are very quick and easy to use, so this is a good card to mass-produce.

 Variation: A photograph of a baby set on a blue or pink background would make a cute card.

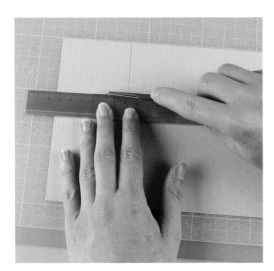

1 If using letter-sized white textured cardstock, trim to 8½" x 5 ¹³⁄₁₆" (21.6 x 14.8cm) (A5). Score and fold to create the card base. Cut a piece of pink cardstock 2½" x 2" (6.5 x 5cm). Use double-sided tape to attach it to a sheet of white cardstock.

2 Cut away all but a narrow frame of white around the pink cardstock. Use double-sided tape to attach this piece to silver cardstock. Once again, cut away all but a narrow border of silver.

4 Using the embossing board and template, emboss a small heart shape in a central position below the framed picture.

3 Adhere the peel-off centrally on the pink cardstock. Use double-sided tape to attach the framed image in an upper central position on the card front.

5 Use pink 3D paint to mark a dot in each corner of the image, slightly outside the frame, to complete the card.

Teddy Bear

New arrival cards are always a pleasure to make, and this card is particularly special with its ribbon and rivet design. Try a pink, lemon yellow, or green background and use other peel-offs to decorate bags, tags, and boxes.

Materials

- Letter/A4 sheet white textured cardstock
- Craft knife
- Metal ruler
- Cutting mat
- Stylus
- Pencil
- Wooden board
- Rivet setting tools
- Hammer
- 6 silver rivets
- Small piece pale blue cardstock
- Double-sided tape
- Scissors
- Small piece silver cardstock
- Silver teddy bear peel-off
- Silver heart sequin
- White glue
- Thin pale blue ribbon

Effort: You need to spend a little time on this card, as it is important to get the rivets positioned evenly and neatly.

Variation: Turn this card into a wedding invitation—use a peel-off to replace the teddy and insert printed invitation details.

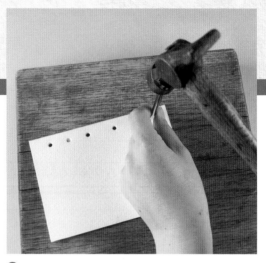

2 Place the card on a wooden board. Use the rivet hole maker and a hammer to make holes at the marked spots.

1 Cut the sheet of white textured A4 cardstock in half (to create two A5 pieces), or, if using US letter paper, cut a piece that is 8½" x 5 ¹³⁄₁₆" (21.6 x 14.8cm) (A5). Score and fold this piece to create the card base and set the other piece aside for now. Measure in ½" (1cm) from the folded spine of the card. Working down the card, mark light pencil dots at ½" (1.5cm), 1½" (4cm), 2½" (6.5cm), 3¼" (8.5cm), 4¼" (11cm), and 5¼" (13.5cm).

3 Press the rivets through the holes. Use a hammer and the rivet placement tool to secure the rivets.

4 Cut out a 1½" x 1¼" (4 x 3.5cm) rectangle from pale blue cardstock. Use double-sided tape to attach this to a piece of textured white cardstock. Cut away all but a narrow frame of white. Tape this onto silver cardstock and cut away all but a narrow frame of silver.

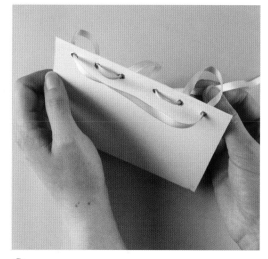

6 Thread the blue ribbon through the rivets and tie a bow.

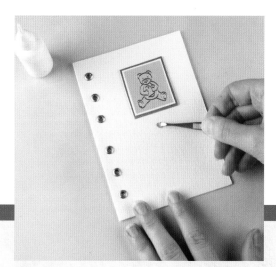

5 Attach the layered piece in an upper central position on the card front. Place the teddy bear peel-off sticker in a central position on the blue cardstock. Glue a small silver heart ½" (1cm) beneath the framed picture.

Witches Abroad

I have used a selection of Halloween-themed premade cutouts on this card. If you cannot find suitable cutouts or want to be even more creative, try creating your own collages using stickers and colored paper.

Decorate goodie bags with motifs and stars. Wrap gifts in corrugated cardstock and make tags using single motifs.

Materials

+ Half letter/A5 sheet black cardstock
+ Craft knife
+ Metal ruler
+ Cutting mat
+ Stylus
+ Black glitter cardstock

+ Double-sided tape
+ Scissors
+ Lime green cardstock
+ Yellow cardstock
+ Halloween cutouts
+ Gold 3D paint
+ Star stickers

Effort: This card is quick to make if you use purchased stickers.

Variation: Try a freehand drawing of a scary spider decorated with 3D paint for a simple card.

1 Cut a 6" x 4½" (15 x 11cm) rectangle from the black cardstock. Score and fold to create the card base. Cut a 1" (2.5cm) square from the black glitter cardstock. Use double-sided tape to attach the square to lime green cardstock. Cut away all but a narrow border of lime green. Then adhere this to yellow cardstock and again cut away all but a narrow border of yellow. Repeat this process to make a second motif.

2 Use double-sided tape to stick the cutouts in position on the two cardstock motifs. Place the central cutout directly on the card first, and then the two finished motifs.

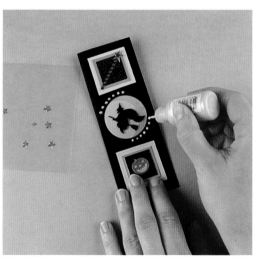

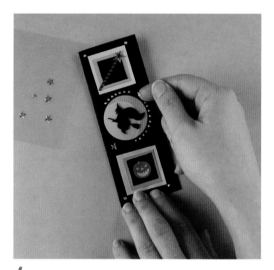

3 Use gold 3D paint to print dots around the central motif—seven on the upper left and ten on the lower right.

4 Print gold dots on the upper corners of the top motif and the lower corners of the bottom motif. Place two star stickers decoratively on the upper right and lower left of the central motif.

HAPPY HALLOWEEN

Celebrate Halloween with this cute collage card. The card is made up of many elements—freehand drawing, rubber stamping, and paper cutouts. You can create many designs using a collage of different materials. Try using stickers as well.

Materials

+ Letter/A4 sheet black cardstock
+ Craft knife
+ Metal ruler
+ Cutting mat
+ Stylus
+ Pencil
+ Double-sided tape
+ Scissors
+ Sheet black glitter cardstock

+ Green, pink, white, and blue gel pens
+ Acetate
+ Sheet white cardstock
+ White glue
+ 2 tiny wiggle eyes
+ Sheet orange cardstock
+ Black fine-tip pen
+ Frog rubber stamp
+ Green stamp pad

Effort: Take some time to practice your freehand drawing before you start making this card.

Variation: Personalize a card with a photo of someone in costume.

2 Draw a white gel pen spiderweb in the top right-hand corner of the card. Draw a spider in the center.

1 Cut the sheet of black A4 cardstock in half (to create two A5 pieces), or, if using US letter paper, cut a piece that is 8½" x 5 ¹³⁄₁₆" (21.6 x 14.8cm) (A5). Score and fold this piece to create the card base and set the other piece aside for now. Cut a 2¾" x 4" (7 x 10cm) rectangle of black cardstock. Use double-sided tape to attach it to a sheet of glitter cardstock. Cut away all but a narrow border of the glitter cardstock. Use double-sided tape to attach this piece centrally on the card base.

3 Trace the ghostly shape on page 218 and cut it out of white cardstock. Use white glue to attach two wiggle eyes. Tape the ghost in the top left-hand corner of the card.

4 Trace the pumpkin templates on page 218 and cut out of orange cardstock. Draw lines on the pumpkins using a black fine-tip pen to give them more dimension.

Spooky fun!

5 Stamp a green frog onto the bottom right-hand corner of the card and use a blue gel pen to draw three ripples around it.

MAGIC NUMBER

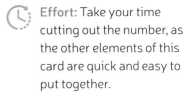

Number motifs brighten up plain white or brown bags wonderfully. I created the handle of the smaller bag shown here using an oval cutter, template, and board.

Number cutouts make great card decorations. This card will work with any number, and there are templates for numbers 0 through 9 on pages 220–222. If the number you want to use is more than one digit, simply reduce the size of the numbers and overlap them slightly on the card to get them all to fit.

Materials

+ Letter/A5 sheet spring green cardstock
+ Metal ruler
+ Stylus
+ Yellow cardstock
+ Cutting mat
+ Craft knife
+ Pencil
+ Double-sided tape
+ Scissors
+ Red cardstock
+ Blue corrugated cardstock
+ Yellow and blue 3D paint
+ Tracing paper/acetate
+ Polka dot wrapping paper
+ White paper (if needed as wrapping paper backing)
+ 3D tape
+ Spring green paper

 Effort: Take your time cutting out the number, as the other elements of this card are quick and easy to put together.

Variation: The sky's the limit—use different wrapping papers to create different effects.

1 If using letter-sized green cardstock, trim to 8½" x 5 ¹³⁄₁₆" (21.6 x 14.8cm) (A5). Score and fold to create the card base. Cut out a 4" x 3" (10 x 8cm) rectangle from the yellow cardstock. Attach it to the card base in an upper central position using double-sided tape.

2 Cut out a 3¾" x 3" (9.5 x 7.5cm) rectangle from the red cardstock. Tape it on top of the yellow cardstock. Cut out a 3½" x 2½" (8.5 x 6.5cm) rectangle of blue corrugated cardstock. Attach this to the red cardstock.

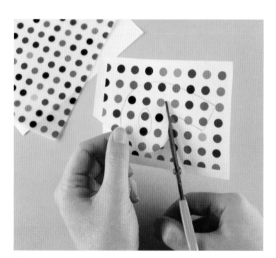

3 Use yellow and blue 3D paint to mark a dotty border on the red frame. Trace the desired number template on pages 220–222. Cut the number out of the wrapping paper. (If you are using translucent wrapping paper, back it with a sheet of white copy paper before cutting out.)

4 Use 3D tape to attach the number to a sheet of green paper. Cut around the number to create a narrow border of green. Use double-sided tape to attach the number centrally on the card.

TIME TO CELEBRATE

There are so many national, international, religious, and just plain fun holidays to celebration all throughout the year. Even if you don't celebrate every holiday featured in this section, you will still be able to take inspiration from the designs to create custom cards for your own holidays. Share the love on each special day!

This card is decorated with an interesting button. For spring greetings, mint green and yellow are a lovely color combination. Look around for other motifs or buttons that would look good with these colors.

Materials

- + Letter/A5 sheet pale green cardstock
- + Metal ruler
- + Stylus
- + Sheet white corrugated cardstock
- + Craft knife
- + Cutting mat
- + Chicken button
- + 3D tape
- + Sheet polka dot paper
- + Double-sided tape
- + Scissors
- + Sheet yellow translucent paper
- + Sheet green translucent paper
- + Daisy punch
- + White glue
- + Yellow 3D paint

 Effort: Set aside an afternoon to make Easter cards for your friends.

 Variation: Look out for interesting buttons and coordinate them with suitable bases.

2 Cut a 2½" (6.5cm) square from polka dot paper. Use double-sided tape to attach the button motif in a central position on the polka dot paper.

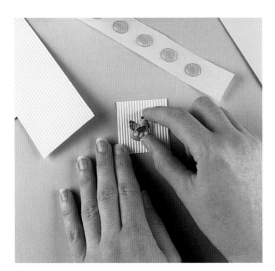

1 If using letter-sized pale green cardstock, trim to 8½" x 5 ¹³⁄₁₆" (21.6 x 14.8cm) (A5). Score and fold to create the card base. Cut a 1¾" (4.5cm) square of white corrugated cardstock. Use 3D tape to attach the button in a central position on the square.

3 Use double-sided tape to attach the piece to a sheet of yellow translucent paper. Cut away all but a narrow frame of yellow. Tape this to a 3¼" (8cm) square of green translucent paper.

4 Attach the layered item in an upper central position on the green card base.

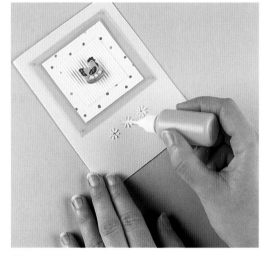

6 Put dots of yellow 3D paint in the corners of the framed picture and in the center of each daisy.

5 Punch out three white daisies and use white glue to attach them in a row beneath the picture.

EASTER BUNNIES

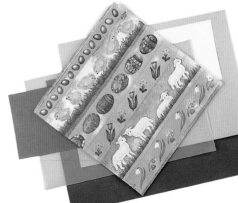

Use paper table napkins and wooden cutouts to make this greeting card. If you cannot find wooden motifs, use stickers or make your own paper cutouts to achieve a similar effect.

Materials

- Letter/A4 sheet yellow cardstock
- Metal ruler
- Pencil
- Craft knife
- Cutting mat
- Stylus
- Half letter/A5 sheet green cardstock
- Double-sided tape
- Scissors
- Half letter/A5 sheet orange cardstock
- Sheet yellow translucent paper
- Half letter/A5 sheet white cardstock
- 3 wooden rabbit cutouts
- Easter paper napkin
- White paper
- Spray adhesive
- Green 3D paint

Effort: Preparing the elements of this card takes a little time.

Variation: Make a card with a nautical theme—use sailboat motifs.

1 Cut a 7¾" x 6" (19.5 x 16cm) rectangle from yellow cardstock. Score and fold it in half so that the card base is in a landscape orientation. Cut a 7½" x 2¾" (19 x 7cm) rectangle of green cardstock and use double-sided tape to attach it to the card base. Cut a 7¼" x 2½" (18.5 x 6.5cm) rectangle of orange cardstock. Use double-sided tape to attach it centrally on the green cardstock.

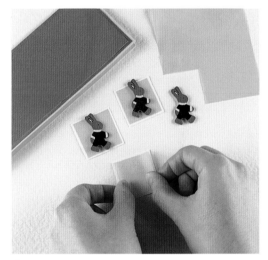

2 Measure and cut out three 1¼" (3.5cm) squares of yellow translucent paper and three 1½" (3.75cm) squares of white cardstock. Use double-sided tape to attach the yellow squares to the white squares. Tape the rabbit motifs centrally on each yellow square.

3 Separate the decorated layer of the napkin from the other layers. Spray a sheet of white paper with spray adhesive and smooth the napkin onto it. Cut out four eggs.

4 Use double-sided tape to attach the three rabbit motifs, positioning the central one first, and the eggs.

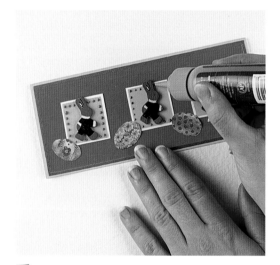

5 Paint a border of tiny dots around the yellow translucent paper squares.

Nest Egg

Three pretty Easter eggs in a delicate gold wire nest adorn this card. I have used embossed stamped images to make the Easter eggs. If you don't have a stamp, cut out small ovals and decorate them with felt-tip pens or colored foil. Use the decorated eggs to make alternative cards and gift tags.

Materials

- Half letter/A5 sheet blue cardstock
- Craft knife
- Cutting mat
- Pencil
- Metal ruler
- Stylus
- Half letter/A5 sheet textured white cardstock
- Corner punch
- Blue and white polka dot paper
- Double-sided tape
- Scissors
- Gold cardstock
- Decorative gold wire
- Super glue
- Embossing pad
- Small Easter egg rubber stamp
- Scrap of white cardstock
- Scrap paper
- Gold embossing powder
- Tweezers or tongs
- Precision heat tool
- Felt-tip pens
- 3D tape

 Effort: Spend a little time preparing the Easter eggs, as they are the feature of the card.

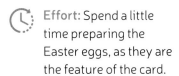 **Variation:** Instead of eggs in a nest, try presents in a box, flowers in a vase, or cakes on a plate.

1 Cut a 6¼" x 5¼" (16 x 13.5cm) rectangle from the blue cardstock. Score and fold to create the card base. Cut a 2¾" x 5" (7 x 12.5cm) rectangle from the white textured cardstock. Use the corner punch to cut decorative corners.

2 Cut out a 3" x 1" (7.5 x 2.5cm) rectangle from the polka dot paper. Use double-sided tape to attach it to gold cardstock. Cut away all but a narrow border of gold. Use double-sided tape to attach the gold-framed polka dot paper in a central position on the white textured cardstock, and then tape the layered piece onto the card base.

4 Use the embossing pad and stamp to print three eggs on a scrap of white cardstock. Fold a sheet of scrap paper in half and open it out. Put the stamped white cardstock on the scrap paper and sprinkle it with gold embossing powder. Shake the excess powder onto the scrap paper and return it to the container. Holding the cardstock with tweezers or tongs, seal the designs with the precision heat tool.

3 Make the nest by wrapping decorative gold wire around two fingers. Wrap the wire around about 10 times. Remove the wire from your fingers, cut, and wrap the ends around the wire oval. Shape into a flattened nest. Glue in place with super glue.

5 Use felt-tip pens to decorate the embossed eggs. Cut them out. Place 3D tape on the backs of the eggs and press into place in the nest.

Delicate spring flowers and pretty ribbon are the main features of this lovely Easter card. You might want to use a different color scheme; try pink and green or powder blue and white with lemon yellow features.

Materials

- + Letter/A5 sheet lilac cardstock
- + Stylus
- + Metal ruler
- + Oval cutter, template, and board
- + Half letter/A5 sheet yellow and lilac polka dot paper
- + Letter/A4 sheet white paper
- + Double-sided tape
- + 2¾" (7cm) of ¾" (1.75cm)–wide pale blue organza ribbon
- + 3¼" (8.5cm) of ½" (1cm)–wide pink organza ribbon

- + Spray adhesive
- + Lilac blue blossom decorated paper
- + Craft knife
- + Cutting mat
- + 3D tape
- + Flower punch
- + Scrap of lilac paper
- + White glue
- + Scrap of yellow paper
- + Yellow and blue 3D paints

Effort: This card is very simple to make, but it does take a little time to assemble all the layers.

Variation: Instead of an egg, wrap a Christmas present with ribbon and decorate with gold stars. Use festive wrapping paper for the layers.

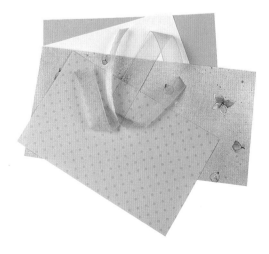

2 Attach a length of double-sided tape across the center of the back of the polka dot egg. Place the blue ribbon across the front of the egg, fold the edges around, and attach them to the double-sided tape on the reverse. Attach the pink ribbon over the blue.

1 If using letter-sized lilac cardstock, trim to 8½" x 5 ¹³⁄₁₆" (21.6 x 14.8cm) (A5). Score and fold to create the card base. To make the egg, use the oval cutter, template, and board to cut a 3" x 2¼" (7.5 x 5.5cm) oval from the polka dot and the white paper. If you do not have an oval cutter, use the template on page 212.

3 Apply spray adhesive on one side of the white oval and attach it to the reverse of the spotted egg. This will help hold the ribbon in position and give the egg some substance. Set the egg aside.

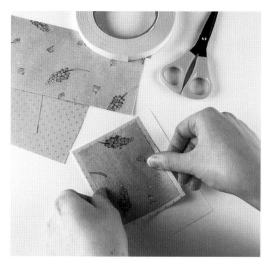

4 Cut a 3" x 3¾" (7.5 x 9.5cm) rectangle from the blossom paper. Use double-sided tape to attach it to polka dot paper; cut away all but a narrow border of polka dot. Layer this onto white paper and, once again, cut away all but a narrow border of white.

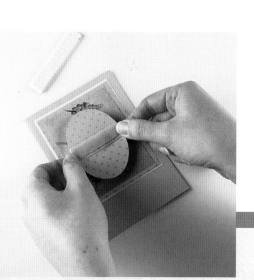

6 Punch out seven small flowers from lilac paper. Use white glue to attach three flowers across the center of the pink ribbon and one in each corner of the frame. Punch out a yellow flower and glue below the layers. Squeeze a dot of yellow 3D paint onto each lilac flower and a blue 3D paint dot onto the yellow flower.

5 Use double-sided tape to attach this piece in an upper central position on the card base. Use 3D tape to attach the egg in a central position on the layers.

CHRISTMAS TREES

This is a stylish Christmas card made from simply decorated paper napkins.

Materials

- Half letter/A5 sheet white cardstock
- Craft knife
- Cutting mat
- Metal ruler
- Pencil
- Stylus
- Decorative paper napkin
- Spray adhesive
- Half letter/A5 sheet white paper
- Scissors
- Double-sided tape
- Small piece red cardstock
- Small piece green cardstock
- Black fine-tip pen

 Effort: This card is reasonably quick to make, so it would be efficient to mass-produce.

 Variation: For a less seasonal look, try this design using a different multi-image paper napkin, perhaps tiny flowers or balloons.

1 Cut an 8" x 4½" (20.5 x 11.5cm) rectangle from the white cardstock. Score and fold to create the card base. Take the napkin and separate out the patterned layer. Discard the plain layers.

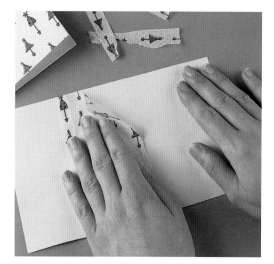

2 Spray the reverse of the patterned layer with spray adhesive. Smooth it over the front of the card base and cut away the excess. Set aside. Adhere the excess of the patterned layer onto a sheet of white paper. Smooth to attach firmly.

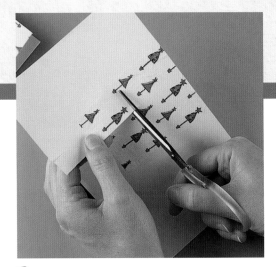

3 Cut out a single tree from the excess patterned piece to be the focal point of your card. Use double-sided tape to attach the feature to a piece of red cardstock. Cut away all but a narrow frame of red.

4 Use double-sided tape to attach the framed image to white cardstock. Cut a 2¼" x 1¾" (6 x 4.5cm) rectangle from the cardstock. Cut a 2½" x 2¾" (6.3 x 7.3cm) rectangle of green cardstock and attach the motif to it. Attach this to red cardstock and cut a narrow frame of red.

Here is a set of seasonal stationery. I've used the central motif on different-colored blanks and layers. You can also use napkins as gift wrap.

5 Attach the layered motif to the card base. Draw a black line around the edge of the white cardstock. Drawn some small stars. You might want to attach a small feature to the back of the card to finish it off.

Robin Redbreast

This robin will bring a little seasonal cheer to a Christmas mantelpiece.

Materials

- Half letter/A5 sheet blue ribbed cardstock
- Craft knife
- Metal ruler
- Cutting mat
- Pencil
- Stylus
- Tracing paper/acetate
- Blue, white, red, brown, and orange foam sheets
- Scissors
- Sheet red cardstock
- Double-sided tape
- Tiny jewel stickers
- Gold star stickers

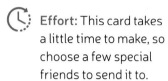

Effort: This card takes a little time to make, so choose a few special friends to send it to.

Variation: Create a country scene with green fields, blue sky, and a white sheep. You could add some fluffy clouds, too.

1 Measure and cut out an 8¼" x 4" (21 x 10.5cm) rectangle of blue ribbed cardstock. Score and fold to create the base.

2 Trace the templates on page 219.

3 Use the templates to cut out the foam shapes for the robin and the background. When cutting the background, cut out a 3½" (8.5cm) square from the blue and white foam sheets. Lay one on top of the other and place the background template on top. Cut through all three layers.

4 Cut a 3¾" (9cm) square of red cardstock. Use double-sided tape to attach the sky and snow background to it. Next, attach the bird body, legs, and hat. Cut the beak from a scrap of orange foam and tape in place.

Use scraps of foam to create your own designs, and use them to decorate cards, tags, and boxes.

5 Stick on the tiny jewel eyes and place the gold star stickers on the blue sky background.

HOLLY BERRIES

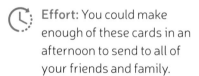

Use similar layered motifs to decorate gift pouches, boxes, and tags. Make your own gift wrap by stamping sprigs of holly onto tissue paper.

Green textured handmade paper and a lovely holly sticker inspired this seasonal card.

Materials

+ Letter/A4 sheet green handmade paper
+ Metal ruler
+ Cutting mat
+ Craft knife
+ Pencil
+ Stylus
+ Small piece gold paper
+ Double-sided tape
+ Scissors
+ Small piece red cardstock
+ Small piece gold cardstock
+ Green angel hair paper
+ Holly sticker

Effort: You could make enough of these cards in an afternoon to send to all of your friends and family.

Variation: Use this design as a starting point, but vary the colors—creams, golds, and earthy colors would look good with a star sticker.

1 Cut an 8¼" x 4¾" (21 x 12cm) square from the handmade paper. Score and fold it to create the card base.

2 Tear out a 3" (7.5cm) square of gold paper. Tape it in a central position on the card so that it is a diamond shape.

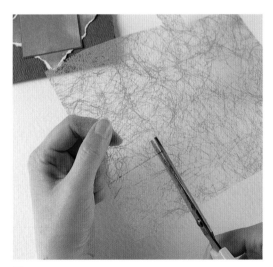

3 Cut a 2½" (6cm) square of red cardstock and attach it with double-sided tape centrally on the gold paper. Cut a 2¼" (5.5cm) square of gold cardstock and tape it on top of the red cardstock. Finally, cut a 2" (5cm) square of angel hair paper and place it on top of the gold cardstock.

4 Place the holly sticker in a central position on the angel hair paper. To give your card a professional finish, place a sticker on the back of the card as well.

WINTER WONDERLAND

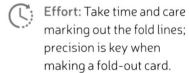

Use the decorated trees to embellish gift bags and tags. Wrap gifts in plain, colored gift wrap and stick on decorated trees.

Stylized Christmas trees adorned with tiny silver jewels decorate this winter scene.

Materials

+ Half letter/A5 sheet silver cardstock
+ Craft knife
+ Metal ruler
+ Cutting mat
+ Pencil
+ Stylus
+ Tracing paper or acetate

+ Half letter/A5 sheet green cardstock
+ Double-sided tape
+ Scissors
+ Tiny silver jewel stickers
+ Red sequin stars
+ White glue

Effort: Take time and care marking out the fold lines; precision is key when making a fold-out card.

Variation: Use this idea to create your own designs. A row of sailing ships or pretty flowers would make lovely cards.

1 Cut an 8¼" x 5" (21 x 13cm) rectangle out of the silver cardstock. On the card front, make light pencil marks at 1½" (3.5cm), 4¼" (10.5cm), and 6⅞" (17.5cm). Score lines at these points. These lines will form the hill folds.

2 Turn the card over and mark points at 2¾" (7cm) and 5½" (14cm). Score lines at these points. These lines will form the valley folds. Fold along all of the lines you have scored to create the card base.

3 Trace the tree templates on page 219. Use them to cut three large trees and four small trees out of green cardstock. Referring to the photograph, position the trees firmly in place using double-sided tape. Pay particular attention to how the trees overlap.

4 Decorate the trees with silver jewel stickers and star sequins. These jewels are tiny and tricky to use, so you may find sliding the jewel off the backing paper works better than lifting it.

STAR BRIGHT

Don't be afraid to use combinations of different materials on your cards. Foil, handmade paper, corrugated cardstock, textured paper, and stickers work well together on this sophisticated seasonal card.

Materials

+ Letter/A5 sheet rich cream textured cardstock
+ Stylus
+ Metal ruler
+ Sheet gold foil
+ Scissors
+ Embossing board and star template
+ Sheet natural handmade paper
+ Sheet brown corrugated cardstock
+ Craft knife
+ Cutting mat
+ Double-sided tape
+ Spray adhesive
+ 3D tape
+ Star stickers

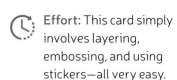 **Effort:** This card simply involves layering, embossing, and using stickers—all very easy.

 Variation: For a housewarming card, emboss a simple house shape and decorate with tiny flower stickers or stamps.

1 If using letter-sized textured cardstock, trim to 8½" x 5 ¹³⁄₁₆" (21.6 x 14.8cm) (A5). Score and fold to create the card base. Cut a 1" (2.5cm) square piece of gold foil. Place it under the star template on the embossing board and use the stylus to emboss the shape. Take your time on this, working over the star image thoroughly so that it will have a good shape.

2 Cut a 2¾" (7cm) square of gold foil; tear two squares of handmade paper, one 2½" (6cm) and the other 1½" (3.5cm); and cut a 1¾" (4.5cm) square of corrugated cardstock. Put double-sided tape on the undersides of the foil and corrugated cardstock and spray the handmade paper squares with spray adhesive.

3 Place the larger piece of gold foil in a high central position on the card base. Next, glue on the larger handmade paper square, followed by the corrugated cardstock, and finally add the smaller handmade paper square. Use 3D tape to attach the embossed star square in a central position. Decorate the card with star stickers.

Make gift bags using the same handmade paper you have used for the card and decorate with the star motif. Print plain gift wrap with a complementary stamped and embossed snowflake design. You can also make alternative cards in other shapes and sizes and decorate them with the same star motif.

HARK THE HERALD ANGELS

Peel-offs usually come on a sheet containing a variety of designs, so use them to decorate other cards, gift wrap, envelopes, and gift pouches.

Here's a sophisticated seasonal card using gold peel-off stickers, cream parchment, and textured paper.

Materials

- Letter/A4 sheet cream textured paper
- Craft knife
- Metal ruler
- Pencil
- Cutting mat
- Letter/A4 sheet plastic sheeting or vellum
- Stylus
- Double-sided tape
- Scissors
- Half letter/A5 sheet cream parchment paper
- Half letter/A5 sheet gold cardstock
- Half letter/A5 sheet cream textured cardstock
- Gold pen
- Angel peel-off sticker
- Gold star stickers

Effort: This card is quick and easy to mass-produce.

Variation: White parchment, vellum, and textured cardstock would look good with silver angels and stars.

1 Cut out a 9½" x 5" (24.5 x 13cm) rectangle of cream textured paper and plastic sheeting. Score and fold the paper and the plastic sheeting.

2 Place two strips of double-sided tape centrally on the inside front cover of the plastic sheeting. Match the fold of the cream paper to the fold of the plastic sheeting and smooth the cream paper onto the front cover of the plastic sheeting.

3 Cut out a 4¼" x 4½" (11 x 11.5cm) piece of cream parchment and use double-sided tape to attach it in a central position on the card front. Cut a 3¾" x 4" (9.5 x 10cm) piece of gold cardstock and tape it on the parchment. Finally, cut a 3½" x 3¾" (9 x 9.5cm) piece of cream textured cardstock. Tape it onto the gold cardstock.

4 Draw thin, gold lines around the edges of the parchment, crossing the corners. Place the angel peel-off sticker centrally on the card. Add a few gold stars to finish the design.

Festive Garland

This card is simple and sophisticated. The clean white cardstock sets off the bright green holly garland and the brilliant red berries.

Materials

+ Half letter/A5 sheet white textured cardstock
+ Pencil
+ Metal ruler
+ Craft knife
+ Cutting mat
+ Stylus
+ Holly leaf punch
+ Green paper
+ Pair of compasses
+ White glue
+ Red 3D paint
+ Red ribbon bow

 Effort: Attaching the holly sprigs can be time-consuming.

 Variation: Make this card in silver and hot pink to create an entirely different mood, or set the holly garland against a rich red background to put a little warmth on a friend's mantelpiece. You might use a sticker or mini Christmas decoration instead of a bow as a feature.

1 Cut a 6¾" x 5½" (17 x 14cm) rectangle from the white textured cardstock. Score and fold in half to create the card base. Punch about 40 holly sprigs from green paper.

2 Lightly draw a 2" (5cm) circle in an upper central position on the card. Squeeze dots of white glue around the circle. Lay the holly sprigs around the circle, working in just one direction, but lean the sprigs to the right and left as you go to create a thick garland.

3 Once the glue is dry, squeeze dots of red 3D paint in groups of two or three around the garland.

4 Attach the ribbon bow with white glue. For a professional finish, you may want to glue a holly sprig on the back of the card and use it to decorate an envelope.

DAISY PUNCH GALLERY

Stylish, simple, and quick to put together, these cards all have a crisp, clean look and were created using the same daisy punch. Punches are easy to use with paper or thin cardstock. I particularly enjoyed using thin cardstock because once the daisies were stuck in place, I was able to raise the petals slightly to create a three-dimensional effect. All of the cards here have been embellished with 3D paint.

1 A white card base provides a stylish background for three red daisies. Punch out the daisies and attach them to a square of cardstock. Cut simple stalks and leaves and use white glue to adhere in place. Layer them over coordinating colors and tape the motif in an upper central position. Embellish with yellow 3D paint.

2 This card is tall and slim; in fact, it would make a good bookmark! Attach the daisies in a zigzag fashion and choose subtle colors for the layers to focus attention on the daisies. Use red and yellow 3D paint to decorate.

3 Using corrugated cardstock gives this design an entirely different look. Stamp and emboss a vase design on thin cardstock. Cut it out and adhere on the corrugated cardstock. The horizontal stripes give the impression of a tablecloth.

4 This card can be displayed horizontally or vertically. The design is simple—white daisies with yellow centers on a blue card base.

5 Another stamped vase graces this card; embellish the pastel shades with silver 3D paint. Using pale colors gives this card an entirely different look from the other cards in this collection.

6 Three daisies in a row are charming. There is something about threes—two is too few, four is too many! This design would look good in almost any color scheme.

7 Once again, a simple design—three daisy motifs, layered and decorated with 3D paint. Use a punch to make the holes for the ribbon. You might want to add an insert on which to write a greeting.

INDIGO BLUE PAPER GALLERY

T he wonderful blue of this striking gift wrap reminded me of Africa, Indonesia, and many other cultures with histories rich in art and design. A single gift wrap pattern can inspire many different card designs.

1 A gift bag is quick and easy to make (see page 36). Tie it with an organza bow and decorate with a special photograph layered on blue cardstock.

2 This little gift tag is simplicity itself: cardstock layers decorated with a craft wire heart.

3 Emboss a simple design onto copper foil. Attach the foil feature to a gift wrap background and frame with thin ribbons of the same paper.

4 Here is a gift tag simply decorated with a single punched flower. Make a hole with a punch and attach a gold tie.

5 Wrap a box in the gift wrap and tie with gold cord.

6 Make a dark blue card base and create a motif made up of three layers—white cardstock, gift wrap, white cardstock. Punch flowers out of finely corrugated cardstock and attach with 3D tape. Draw the stems with green 3D paint.

7 I used the wrapping paper design to my advantage on this card. Form a grid of white paper ribbons and draw a flower with white 3D paint.

8 Blue handmade paper and yellow cardstock give this greeting card a very different feel from the rest of the collection. Embellish the gift wrap with yellow 3D paint.

Peacock Feather Stamp Gallery

This stamp is stylish, simple, and so inspirational. Purchasing a stamp can stretch your budget, but they are incredibly versatile, as this gallery shows.

1 Emboss a pink feather on vellum and edge with green glitter. Attach the design to a red handmade paper base.

2 Use yellow cardstock as a base. Cut a frame of yellow angel hair paper, with a wider area at the bottom. Stamp the feather onto the card and emboss in gold. Decorate with gold glitter.

3 Stamp the feather onto black cardstock and emboss in baby pink. Edge the tag with baby pink embossing powder. Punch a hole in the end and thread with pink ribbon.

4 Stamp the feather onto vellum and emboss in red glitter. Cut out the design and back with white cardstock. Layer onto vellum and red cardstock. Attach the motif to a white card base.

5 Color the stamp with blue, purple, and green felt-tip pens. Stamp onto a piece of patterned white paper. Cut into a diamond shape and back with silver cardstock.

6 Stamp the image onto vellum and cut out. Attach to white, textured cardstock. Leaving a fairly wide border, trim with deckle-edged scissors. Tape the motif slightly to the right of a pink card base. Punch two holes at the left edge, thread pink ribbon through the holes, and tie a bow.

7 Decorate a white gift pouch. Use a scrap of paper to cover the part of the stamp that you do not want on the printed image.

8 Color the stamp with purple, green, and blue felt-tip pens. Back the stamped image in white cardstock and layer on top of gold, purple, and dark blue cardstock. Attach the motif to a white card base with 3D tape.

9 Color the stamp with felt-tip pens as before and stamp onto vellum. Back with a small rectangle of white cardstock. Highlight with a border of gold paper ribbons and silver 3D paint.

Paper Rosebuds Gallery

Red roses signify romance, while pink roses carry loving thoughts. White roses lend themselves to serenity, making them more suited to cards with deep, emotional messages. Rosebuds can be tied to simply wrapped gifts; you might want to use freshly-picked rosebuds to carry a special romantic message. To create coordinating gift wrap, stamp roses onto tissue paper, stencil them onto colored paper, and emboss buds on brown paper.

1 Here is a simply wrapped gift: red tissue paper decorated with red rosebuds and tied with green ribbon.

2 This white card base shows a layered feature. Attach the rosebuds to a rectangle of white cardstock covered with green angel hair paper. Tie with a bow sticker. Surround the design with gold 3D paint dots.

3 Wrap a bunch of paper roses in tissue paper and attach to subtly colored cardstock layers.

4 Hearts and flowers—what more could a loved one ask for? Cut a heart-shaped frame out of red cardstock. Attach the flowers and tie with a silver bow. Finish off the design with dots of red 3D paint.

5 Photocopy a suitable photograph onto acetate. Cut out a section and layer it onto white cardstock. Attach the bunch of roses and tie with a ribbon of red cardstock.

Stickers, peel-offs, and cutouts are used here to good effect. The range of stickers available is almost endless, so you can decorate a gift for any occasion and personalize it for the recipient. Peel-offs and stickers are best attached once the gift is wrapped; this way you can place them where they will not be covered by the ribbon.

1 and **2** You will need suitable champagne bottle and glass party sequins. Scatter tiny dots of white glue on violet paper, bearing in mind the pattern that you want to create with the sequins. Add the sequins. Use pretty ribbon to finish off the parcel.

3 This gift wrap is so quick and easy to make. Simply decorate a sheet of deep blue tissue paper with peel-off gold stars.

4 These red cracker, gold streamer, and star stickers on white tissue paper create a sophisticated look. Tie the gift with green starry ribbon for a seasonal feel.

5 I cut these pumpkins from a Halloween streamer. The orange pumpkins look great on the green background, and the tiny star stickers add a little magic to the paper. Use white glue to attach the motifs.

6 These ghosts were cut from a Halloween streamer, too. Use white glue to attach them. Decorate a gift wrapped in this paper with an orange ribbon bow.

7 Decorate a brown paper bag with a layered motif. Cut a square of green tissue paper and use spray adhesive to attach it to a square of gold cardstock. Layer this onto green and then orange cardstock. Decorate with pumpkins and gold star stickers.

RUBBER STAMPS GALLERY

Card makers are now spoiled for choice when it comes to rubber stamps. If you decorate a card with a stamp, you might want to use the same stamp to decorate tissue paper or a gift bag, box, or pouch. Making a set of coordinating items couldn't be simpler. If you want to be a little more adventurous, emboss the stamped design using embossing powders and seal using a precision heat tool (see page 25).

1 Stamp Christmas puddings in gold onto bright red tissue paper. Emboss with gold embossing powder and seal with a precision heat tool. This stamped design would also look good if stamped and embossed in a bright red or green on brown paper.

2 I haven't actually used a rubber stamp here! Simply use dots of 3D paint running in a freehand design to create a decorative pattern. You could use a simple rubber stamp to create a similar effect.

3 Stamp bright yellow tissue paper with a candle design. Emboss the designs with bronze embossing powder and seal with a precision heat tool. Color with felt-tip pens. Use a plain layer of tissue paper beneath the decorated layer so that the present inside is completely concealed.

4 and **5** White daisies on a sky blue background give a fresh country feel. Stamp the daisy in white, sprinkle with white embossing powder, and seal with a precision heat tool. Draw the leaves using an embossing pen, sprinkle with green embossing powder, and seal. Put a dot of yellow 3D paint in the center of each daisy. Finish the present off with a blue and white gingham ribbon bow.

6 and **7** Here is a very different look created with the same daisy stamp as used on items 4 and 5. Hot pink tissue paper printed with white daisies is great for a fashionable friend's birthday gift. Use a gauze ribbon to tie up the package.

STENCILS GALLERY

Create your own stencil by drawing a simple shape onto cardstock and cutting it out using a craft knife. An even simpler way to make a stencil is to use a punch to cut a shape from the cardstock. You can use an ink dauber, stamp pad, embossing powders (sealed using a precision heat tool; see page 25), or paint to color the design.

1 This is a sophisticated design in black and white. Use a flower punch to create the stencil. Print the design using a clear stamp pad, sprinkle with white embossing powder, and seal using a precision heat tool. Put a dot of 3D paint in the center of each flower.

2 The same stencil used on item 1 has been used here to create quite a different effect. Stencil the summery yellow tissue paper using a purple stamp pad. Use clear embossing powder to give the flowers a special finish. Seal using a precision heat tool. Put a dot of yellow 3D paint in the center of each flower.

3 This wrapping paper has been decorated using the same stencil used on items 1 and 2. This time, stencil and emboss red flowers onto white tissue paper.

4 and **5** Create a star stencil by drawing a star onto thin cardstock and cutting it out with a craft knife, or use a star punch. Stamp the star shape onto the blue tissue paper using a clear stamp pad and then emboss using silver embossing powder. Seal using a precision heat tool.

6 Stencil hot pink tissue paper in exactly the same way as described for items 4 and 5. A silver ribbon would look good with this paper.

7 Multi-colored stars created with the same star stencil as used for items 4, 5, and 6 brighten up a sheet of yellow tissue paper. Stencil the stars in different colors and use clear embossing powder to give them a shiny finish.

8 Follow the instructions for items 4 and 5, but use gold embossing powder on red tissue paper instead.

9 Buy a plain, colored gift bag and decorate it with stenciled stars. If you are unable to buy a bag in the color that you want, simply make one following the instructions on page 36.

HANDMADE PAPER GALLERY

Making Your Own Greeting Cards & Gift Wrap

There are so many beautiful handmade papers available to tempt the card maker. Plain, colored, or textured paper provides a good base for stamping or stenciling, and narrow bands of paper containing leaves, flowers, and other decorative features are just wonderful for embellishing gifts.

1 Take turquoise handmade paper as a base. Use an embossing pen to mark some very simple branch shapes. Emboss with brown embossing powder and seal with a precision heat tool (see page 25). Punch out small pink flower shapes. Use white glue to attach the flowers to the branches in groups of two or three and also scatter a few randomly between the branches. Paint a spot of pink 3D paint in the center of each flower and dot green 3D paint around the flowers to represent leaves. Finally, tie a green ribbon around the finished package.

2 Stamp daisies onto white tissue paper using a clear stamp pad, and then emboss them with pink embossing powder and seal with a precision heat tool (see page 25). Use a leaf stamp or draw leaves freehand with an embossing pen. Emboss with green embossing powder and seal.

3 Wrap a gift in red handmade paper and place a band of white decorative paper around it. Finish with a small bunch of paper rosebuds attached using white glue. This would be perfect wrapping for a Valentine's Day gift.

4 Make a small gift bag from pumpkin yellow handmade paper (following the instructions for making gift bags on page 36). Punch holes through the top of the bag and thread with a fine cord tie. Decorate the bag with a sprig of paper bamboo leaves.

5 Wrap a gift in pink silver-threaded handmade paper and decorate with a band of white textured paper. Embellish with pink ribbon and a sprig of paper leaves and flowers.

6 This present has a simple country feel. Wrap a gift in green handmade paper, then attach a length of gingham ribbon around the center of the gift. Cut heart shapes out of red handmade paper and adhere onto the ribbon.

TEMPLATES

The templates shown here are actual size unless otherwise stated. They may be easily enlarged or reduced on a photocopier if you wish to make a larger or smaller card.

Gift pouch (page 34)

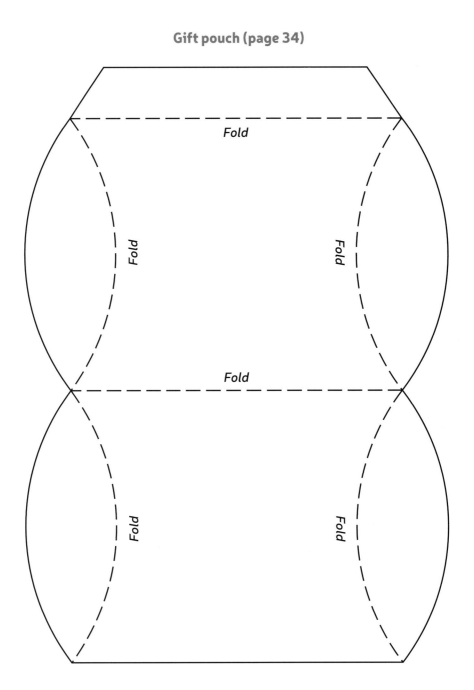

Bead Dolly (page 64)

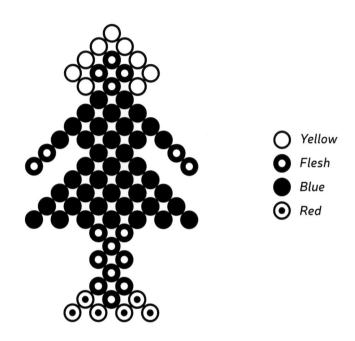

○ Yellow
◉ Flesh
● Blue
◉ Red

How Does Your Garden Grow? (page 48)

Olive Branch (page 66)

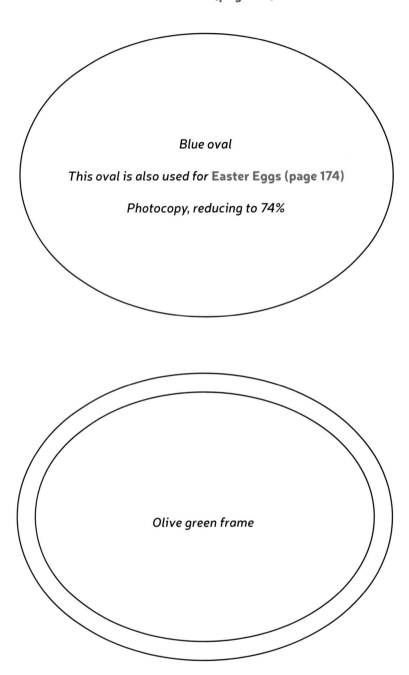

Blue oval

This oval is also used for **Easter Eggs (page 174)**

Photocopy, reducing to 74%

Olive green frame

Olive Branch (page 66)

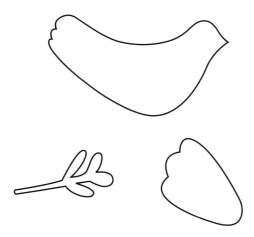

Bookmark (page 70)

Memories (page 74)

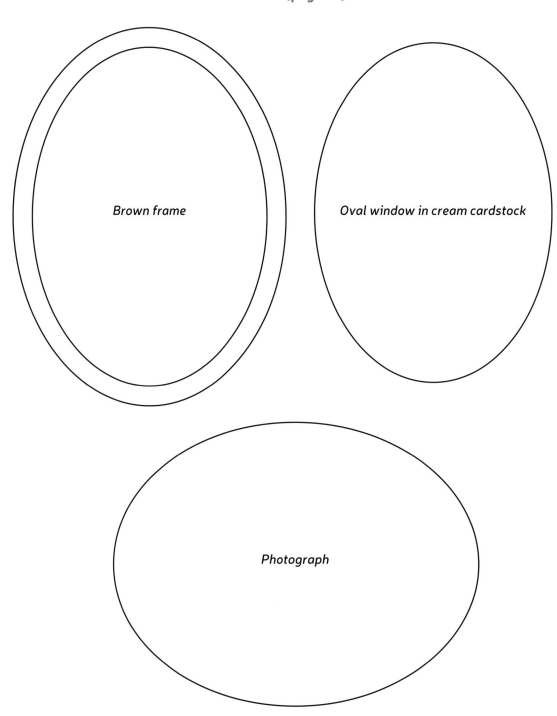

Brown frame

Oval window in cream cardstock

Photograph

Funky Foam Flowers (page 106)

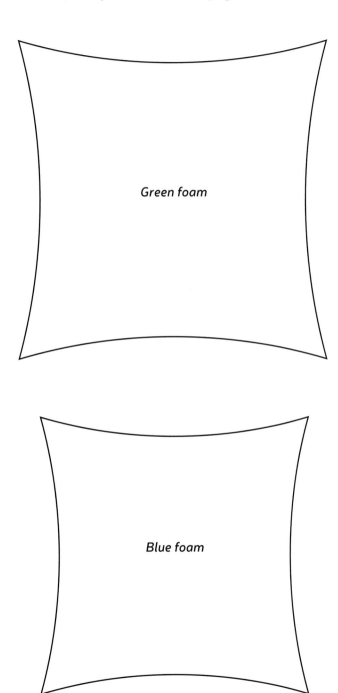

Green foam

Blue foam

Funky Foam Flowers (page 106)

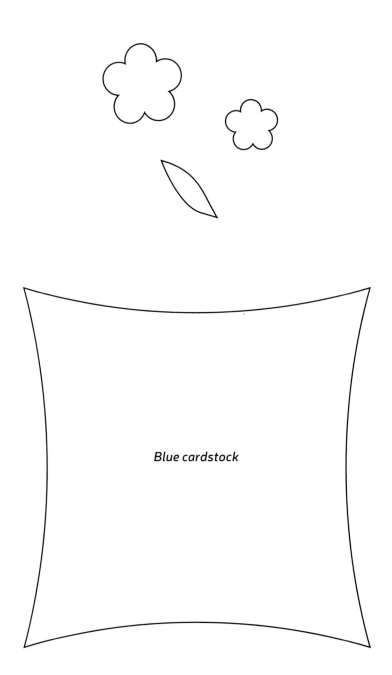

Blue cardstock

Patchwork House (page 124)

Sparkling Hearts (page 129)

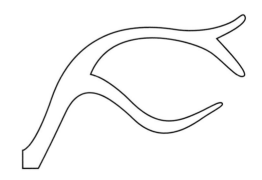

Cherry Blossom (page 112)

Wedding Cake (page 138)   **Tiny Onesie (page 144)**

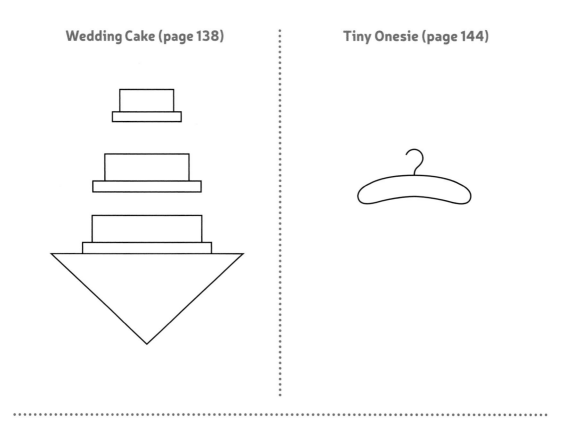

Happy Halloween (page 156)

Winter Wonderland (page 186)

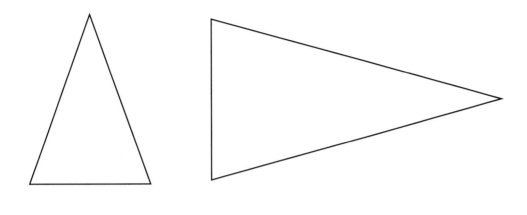

Robin Redbreast (page 181)

Magic Number (page 160)

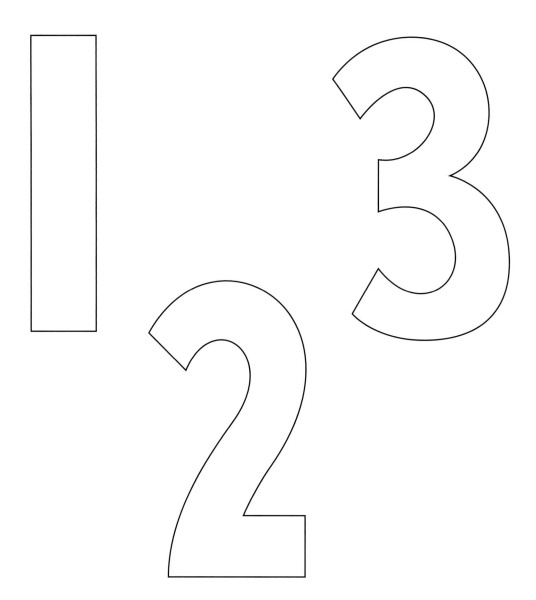

Magic Number (page 160)

INDEX

Photo Credits

Shutterstock.com

Front cover and page 9 photo: Adamova Mariya; back cover pink background: natrot; drop capitals used on back cover and throughout book: passion artist; texture on tops and bottoms of pages 44, 45, and similar: BlurryMe; colored banners used for title, section names, project names, and gallery names on pages 1, 5, 10, 40, 194, 210, front cover, and similar: Khvost; photo page 12: Roman Rybaleov; photo page 14: Piotr Kuczek; photo page 16: Marythepooh; photo page 23: Elena Schweitzer; photo page 29, 224: Antonina Sotnykova

Flaticon.com

Effort and Variation icons for all projects